CUSTOM CURRICULUM

Extreme Friendship

Kara Eckmann Powell

teacher training by
Duffy Robbins

options by
Rev. Nelson Copeland, Jr., Saundra Hensel, Ellen Larson, Jim Marian, Paul Miller, Mark Oestreicher, Darrell Pearson, Susie Shellenberger, and Joel Walker

Cook Ministry Resources
a division of Cook Communications Ministries
Colorado Springs, Colorado/Paris, Ontario

Custom Curriculum
Extreme Friendship

Series Creator: John Duckworth

Editor: Rick Wesselhoff

Series Designer: Bill Paetzold

Additional design: Sonya Duckworth, Erica Whitcombe

Cover and Inside Illustrator: Kathy Badonsky

Special thanks to Mark Oestreicher and Paul Miller for additional ideas, and to Saundra Hensel, who wrote the paraphrase of the Good Samaritan on pages 18-19.

Printed in U.S.A.

www.cookministries.com

Cook Ministry Resources
a division of
Cook Communications Ministries
4050 Lee Vance View,
Colorado Springs, CO
80918-7100

ISBN: 0-7814-5460-3

The Custom Curriculum Challenge

We Challenge You to ...

Refuse "canned" curriculum.

Don't be boxed into one way of doing things.

Think about your group.

How do your students learn best? What kinds of goals do you have for your group? You know what will work with your students.

Reach your teens.

Don't just fill up an hour of programming.

It takes a few minutes each week to customize your curriculum. But if you're willing to take the challenge, the pay off is lessons that work—not just on paper but with real, live teens. With *your* teens.

CONTENTS

About the Authors

Kara Eckmann Powell

5 sessions, Combined options

In her spare time after writing, speaking, and studying for her Doctorate in Practical Theology, Kara is the part-time college pastor at Lake Avenue Congregational Church in Pasadena. Her books include *The Word on the Old Testament* (with Jim Burns). Her strengths include the ability to make abstract truths concrete for teens.

Paul Miller

Small Group, Mostly Guys options

Paul oversees the guys and small-group ministries at Son Light, the 1,000-student middle school ministry of Willow Creek Community Church. He has written youth curriculum at Willow Creek for over 10 years. He believes that every large youth ministry needs a small-group program and every small youth ministry has a built-in advantage, because "Small groups are where life change happens."

Saundra Hensel

Mostly Girls options

Saundra's youth work experience includes stints at Willow Creek and Cedar Ridge Community Church in suburban Washington, D.C. She contributed to the books *Breaking the Gender Barrier in Youth Ministry* and *Reaching a Generation for Christ.* Saundra is the vice-president of the Association of Women in Youth Ministry.

Joel Walker

Extra Action options

Joel runs Peak 3, a high adventure ropes course and initiative games ministry center in Colorado Springs that draws visitors from around the U.S. Joel is a 15-year veteran of youth ministry and an expert in "adventure discipleship"—using initiative games and outdoor learning for Christian ministry.

Ellen Larson

Sixth Grade options

Ellen is an educator and writer with degrees in education and theology. She has served as minister of Christian education in several churches. Her experience also includes teaching in public schools. She is the author of several books for both children and teachers, including the *Value Builders* series of children's books.

Mark Oestreicher

Extra Fun, Large Group options

After leading youth ministries in Omaha and Detroit, Mark now leads a large middle school ministry in Pasadena. He is well known throughout the country as the creator of many wild, fun ideas for young teens. His many books include *Wild Truth Bible Lessons* and four titles in the *Custom Curriculum* series.

Darrell Pearson

Heard It All Before, Media options

Darrell is the producer/presenter of *Wild Truth*, a three-hour event that uses cutting edge media and audience participation to reach junior highers in over 100 cities internationally each year. His many books include *Creative Programming from A to Z* (with Steve Dickie). His 20 years of experience make him one of the true veterans of junior high ministry.

Susie Shellenberger

Mostly Girls options

Susie is a nationally-known youth speaker and the editor of *Brio,* Focus on the Family's monthly magazine for preteen girls. Her books include *Getting Ready for the Guy/Girl Thing* and *What Hollywood Won't Tell You About Sex, Love, and Dating* (both with Greg Johnson). Before *Brio,* Susie was a high school speech and drama teacher and a youth minister.

Jim Marian

Fellowship and Worship options

Jim is an expert on teaching teens how to worship. His books include *Worship Services for Youth Groups* and *Leading Your Students in Worship.* In addition, he has led many retreats, conferences, and training seminars. He has 15 years of youth work experience.

Rev. Nelson Copeland, Jr.

Urban options

Nelson is the President of the Christian Education Coalition for African-American Leadership, an organization dedicated to reinforcing educational and cultural excellence among urban teenagers. His books include *Great Games for City Kids* and *A New Agenda for Urban Youth.* He has 13 years of urban youth ministry experience.

How to Customize Your Curriculum

All right, you may be thinking. With all of these options flying around, how do I put a session together? I don't have a lot of time, you know. We know! That's why we've made Custom Curriculum as easy as possible. Just follow these four steps.

1 Read the basic lesson plan.

Every Custom Curriculum session in this book has five steps designed to meet five goals. The better you understand these five goals the better you'll understand how to choose options that meet these goals.

GETTING TOGETHER
The goal for Getting Together *is to break the ice. It may involve a fun way to introduce the lesson.*

GETTING THIRSTY
The goal for Getting Thirsty *is to earn students' interest before you dive into the Bible. Why should students care about your topic? Why should they care what the Bible has to say about it? This will motivate your students to dig deeper.*

GETTING THE WORD
The goal for Getting the Word *is to find out what God has to say about a topic they care about. By exploring and discussing carefully-selected passages, you'll help students find out how God's Word applies to their lives.*

GETTING THE POINT
The goal for Getting the Point *is to make the leap from ideals and principles to real-world situations students are likely to face. It may involve practicing biblical principles with case studies or roleplays.*

GETTING PERSONAL
The goal for Getting Personal *is to help each group member respond to the lesson with a specific action. What should group members do as a result of this session? This step will help each person find a specific "next step" response that works for him or her.*

2 Know your options.

Every Custom Curriculum session includes 14 different categories of options. How do you choose? First, spend some time thinking and praying about your group. How do your students learn best? What kind of goals have you set for your group? Then take a look at the list of option categories below. Decide which options categories will best meet your needs. You may want to circle or underline your choices on this page.

Extra Action—for groups that like physical challenges and that learn better when they're moving, interacting, and experiencing the lesson.

Media—for groups that will respond well to video, music, or other popular media.

Heard It All Before—to use if you need fresh approaches to get past the defenses of students who may be "jaded" by years in church.

Little Bible Background—to use when most of your students are strangers to the Bible or haven't yet made a Christian commitment.

Extra Fun—for longer, more "festive" youth meetings where additional emphasis is put on having fun.

Fellowship and Worship—for building deeper relationships or enabling students to praise God together.

Mostly Girls—to address girls' concerns and to substitute activities girls might prefer.

Mostly Guys—to address guys' concerns and to substitute activities guys might prefer.

Small Group—for adapting activities that would be tough for groups of fewer than eight students.

Large Group—to alter steps for groups of more than 20 students.

Urban—for fitting sessions to urban facilities and multiethnic (especially African-American) concerns.

Short Meeting Time—for condensing the meeting. The typical meeting is designed to last 45 to 60 minutes. These options include ways to cut, replace, or trim time off the standard steps.

Combined Junior High/High School—to use when you're mixing age levels but an activity or case study would be too "young" or "old" for part of the group.

Sixth Grade Options—appearing only in junior high/middle school volumes, this option helps you change steps that sixth graders might find hard to understand or relate to.

Extra Challenge Options—appearing only in high school volumes, these options let you crank up the voltage for students who are ready for more Scripture or more demanding personal application.

3 Find your options.

Did you make a short list of the options you're most interested in? Great. Now you're ready to customize your curriculum. We've included a sample lesson page here. The side notes will show you just how easy it is to find the options you're looking for.

This sidebar shows you which options are available for Step 3.

This paragraph gives you a brief summary of the standard Step 3.

These page numbers tell you where you can find the options for Step 3.

New Feature! Each Bible Bytes box (there's one in every lesson) provides the background info and additional Scripture references you need to customize your own Bible study.

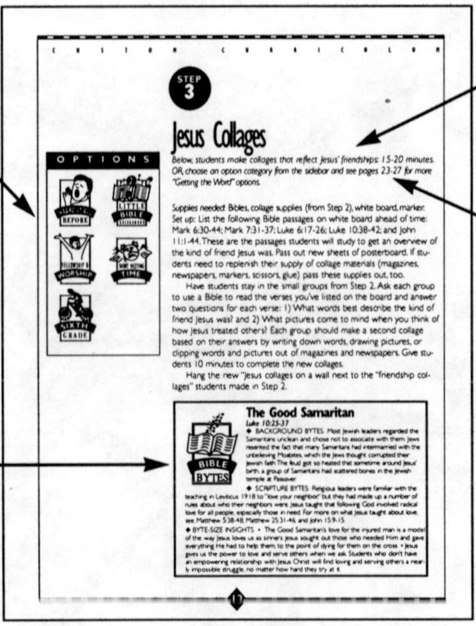
C U S T O M C U R R I C U L U M

STEP 3

Jesus Collages

OPTIONS

Below, students make collages that reflect Jesus' friendships: 15-20 minutes. OR, choose an option category from the sidebar and see pages 23-27 for more "Getting the Word" options.

Supplies needed: Bibles, collage supplies (from Step 2), white board, marker. Set up: List the following Bible passages on white board ahead of time: Mark 6:30-44; Mark 7:31-37; Luke 6:17-26; Luke 10:38-42; and John 11:1-44. These are the passages students will study to get an overview of the kind of friend Jesus was. Pass out new sheets of posterboard. If students need to replenish their supply of collage materials (magazines, newspapers, markers, scissors, glue) pass these supplies out, too.

Have students stay in the small groups from Step 2. Ask each group to use a Bible to read the verses you've listed on the board and answer two questions for each verse: 1) What words best describe the kind of friend Jesus was? and 2) What pictures come to mind when you think of how Jesus treated others? Each group should make a second collage based on their answers by writing down words, drawing pictures, or clipping words and pictures out of magazines and newspapers. Give students 10 minutes to complete the new collages.

Hang the new "Jesus collages on a wall next to the "friendship collages" students made in Step 2.

The Good Samaritan
Luke 10:25-37

◆ BACKGROUND BYTES: Most Jewish leaders regarded the Samaritans unclean and chose not to associate with them. Jews resented the fact that many Samaritans had intermarried with the unbelieving Moabites, which the Jews thought corrupted their Jewish faith. The feud got so heated that sometime around Jesus' birth, a group of Samaritans had scattered bones in the Jewish temple at Passover.

◆ SCRIPTURE BYTES: Religious leaders were familiar with the teaching in Leviticus 19:18 to "love your neighbor" but they had made up a number of rules about who their neighbors were. Jesus taught that following God involved radical love for all people, especially those in need. For more on what Jesus taught about love, see Matthew 5:38-48, Matthew 25:31-46, and John 15:9-15.

◆ BYTE-SIZE INSIGHTS: • The Good Samaritan's love for the injured man is a model of the way Jesus loves us as sinners. Jesus sought out those who needed Him and gave everything He had to help them, to the point of dying for them on the cross. • Jesus gives us the power to love and serve others when we ask. Students who don't have an empowering relationship with Jesus Christ will find loving and serving others a nearly impossible struggle, no matter how hard they try at it.

17

4 Choose the options that will work for you.

When you turn to the back of each session, you'll see five options pages that look something like this.

Find the icon for the option in which you're interested.

You may be able to tell just by reading the subtitle if this is an option you want to use or not.

Use this checklist (there's one in the back of every session) to keep track of the options you've chosen.

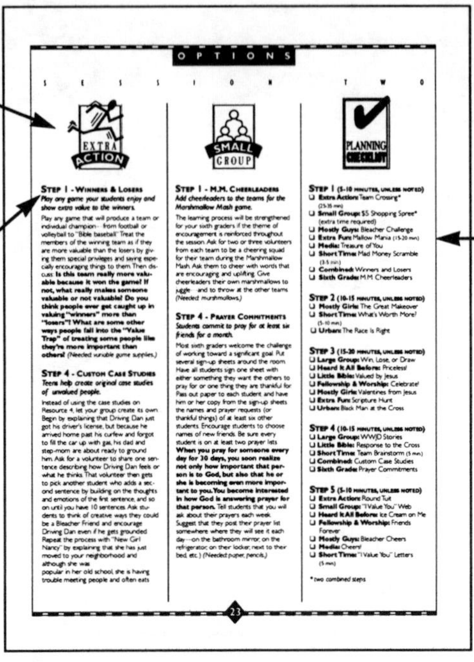
OPTIONS

S E S S I O N T W O

STEP 1 - WINNERS & LOSERS
Play any game your students enjoy and show extra value to the winners.

Play any game that will produce a team or individual champion—from football or volleyball to "Bible baseball." Treat the members of the winning team as if they are more valuable than the losers by giving them special privileges and saying especially encouraging things to them. Then discuss: **Is this team really more valuable because it won the game? If not, what really makes someone valuable or not valuable? Do you think people ever get caught up in valuing "winners" more than "losers"? What are some other ways people fall into the "Value Trap" of treating some people like they're more important than others?** *(Needed: variable game supplies.)*

STEP 4 - CUSTOM CASE STUDIES
Teens help create original case studies of unvalued people.

Instead of using the case studies on Resource 4, let your group create its own. Begin by explaining that Driving Dan just got his driver's license, but because he arrived home past his curfew and forgot to fill the car up with gas, his dad and step-mom are about ready to ground him. Ask for a volunteer to share one sentence describing how Driving Dan feels or what he thinks. That volunteer then gets to pick another student who adds a second sentence by building on the thoughts and emotions of the first sentence, and so on until you have 10 sentences. Ask students to think of creative ways they could be a Bleacher Friend and encourage Driving Dan even if he gets grounded. Repeat the process with "New Girl Nancy" by explaining that she has just moved to your neighborhood and although she was popular in her old school, she is having trouble meeting people and often eats

STEP 1 - M.M. CHEERLEADERS
Add cheerleaders to the teams for the Marshmallow Mash game.

The learning process will be strengthened for your sixth graders if the theme of encouragement is reinforced throughout the session. Ask for two or three volunteers from each team to be a cheering squad for their team during the Marshmallow Mash. Ask them to cheer with words that are encouraging and uplifting. Give cheerleaders their own marshmallows to juggle—and to throw at the other teams. *(Needed: marshmallows.)*

STEP 4 - PRAYER COMMITMENTS
Students commit to pray for at least six friends for a month.

Most sixth graders welcome the challenge of working toward a significant goal. Put several sign-up sheets around the room. Have all students sign one sheet with either something they want the others to pray for or one thing they are thankful for. Pass out paper to each student and have him or her copy from the sign-up sheets the names and prayer requests (or thankful things) of at least six other students. Encourage students to choose names of new friends. Be sure every student is on at least two prayer lists. **When you pray for someone every day for 30 days, you soon realize not only how important that person is to God, but also that he or she is becoming even more important to you. You become interested in how God is answering prayer for that person.** Tell students that you will ask about their prayers each week. Suggest that they post their prayer list somewhere where they will see it each day—on the bathroom mirror, on the refrigerator, on their locker, next to their bed, etc.) *(Needed: paper, pencils.)*

PLANNING CHECKLIST

STEP 1 (5-10 MINUTES, UNLESS NOTED)
- ❑ **Extra Action:** Team Crossing* (25-35 min)
- ❑ **Small Group:** $5 Shopping Spree* (extra time required)
- ❑ **Mostly Guys:** Bleacher Challenge
- ❑ **Extra Fun:** Mallow Mania (15-20 min)
- ❑ **Media:** Treasure of You
- ❑ **Short Time:** Mad Money Scramble (3-5 min)
- ❑ **Combined:** Winners and Losers
- ❑ **Sixth Grade:** M.M. Cheerleaders

STEP 2 (10-15 MINUTES, UNLESS NOTED)
- ❑ **Mostly Girls:** The Great Makeover
- ❑ **Short Time:** What's Worth More? (5-10 min)
- ❑ **Urban:** The Race Is Right

STEP 3 (15-20 MINUTES, UNLESS NOTED)
- ❑ **Large Group:** Win, Lose, or Draw
- ❑ **Heard It All Before:** Priceless!
- ❑ **Little Bible:** Valued by Jesus
- ❑ **Fellowship & Worship:** Celebrate!
- ❑ **Mostly Girls:** Valentines from Jesus
- ❑ **Extra Fun:** Scripture Hunt
- ❑ **Urban:** Black Man at the Cross

STEP 4 (10-15 MINUTES, UNLESS NOTED)
- ❑ **Large Group:** WWJD Stories
- ❑ **Little Bible:** Response to the Cross
- ❑ **Short Time:** Team Brainstorm (5 min)
- ❑ **Combined:** Custom Case Studies
- ❑ **Sixth Grade:** Prayer Commitments

STEP 5 (5-10 MINUTES, UNLESS NOTED)
- ❑ **Extra Action:** Round Tuit
- ❑ **Small Group:** "I Value You" Web
- ❑ **Heard It All Before:** Ice Cream on Me
- ❑ **Fellowship & Worship:** Friends Forever
- ❑ **Mostly Guys:** Bleacher Cheers
- ❑ **Media:** Cheers!
- ❑ **Short Time:** "I Value You" Letters (5 min)

* two combined steps

23

Publicity Clip Art

The images on these two pages are designed to help you promote this course within your church and community. Feel free to photocopy anything here and adapt it to fit your publicity needs. This page could be used as a flyer that you send or hand out to kids—or as a bulletin insert. The art on the next page could be used to add visual interest to newsletters, calendars, bulletin boards, or other promotions. Be creative and have fun!

Are You Ready For Extreme Friendship?

You've heard of extreme sports like bungee jumping and luge running. But what is Extreme Friendship? It's not just being nice. It's more than saying, "I'll be there for you." It's all about being the kind of self-sacrificing, life-laying-down friend-in-action that JESUS is to us. Are you ready for this?

Where:

When:

Questions? Call:

Life's short. Cheer hard.
Be a **BLEACHER FRIEND.**

Friends don't let friendships die quietly. Will you be a **SECOND-CHANCE** Friend?

Get off the couch. Get into somebody's life.
Be a **FOXHOLE FRIEND.**

Will you **FORGIVE?**

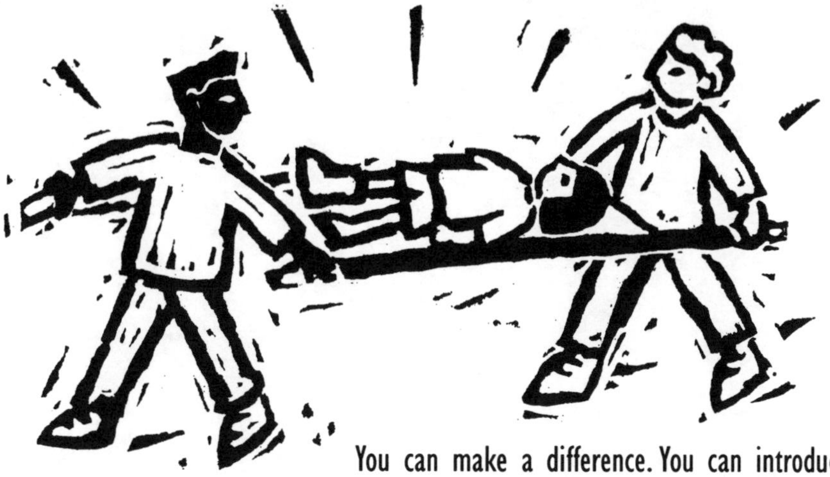

You can make a difference. You can introduce your friends to Jesus. You can step up and be a **STRETCHER FRIEND.**

Teacher Training

Friendship, Fellowship, and Shipwrecked Relationships

Talking to Young Teens About Friendship

by Duffy Robbins

> The long shadows dancing in the trees around our campfire were swaying to the familiar tune, "Friends are friends forever if the Lord's the Lord of them, and a friend cannot say never 'cause the welcome will not end. Though it's hard to let them go, in the Father's hands we know that a lifetime's not to long (sniff, sniff, wipe tears away) . . . to live as friends."
>
> *("Friends," Michael W. Smith)*

It was one of those magic camp night moments when the kids were holding hands, staring into the fire, and feeling the warmth of being together in the presence of God's Spirit. I thought to myself, "Thank you, Lord. Thank you for the way you're working among these kids; thank you for giving my students this taste of genuine fellowship . . . and thank you that they didn't decide to sing 'Pass It On!' "

It wasn't cynicism that ushered me to my next thought; it was the realism that comes with over two decades of youth ministry. Glancing around at the golden, glowing faces I thought, "If only we could make this moment last . . . at least until we all finish the bus ride home tomorrow!"

WE'RE ONE IN SPIRIT . . . BUT I'M NUMBER ONE IN REAL LIFE.

I can't really condemn the kids for the struggles they have in maintaining healthy relationships. Building community is tough. Authentic friendship is hard work. "Extreme Friendship" is extremely difficult. You don't have to be a teenager to relate to the words of the old hymn:

> "To dwell above with saints we love, O that will be glory!
> But to dwell below with the saints we know, that's another story."

And yet, this is our mandate, and one of the primary ways by which we can prove to the watching world that we are followers of the Lord Jesus. There certainly was nothing neat, easy, and clean about Jesus' act of servanthood that night in the upper room when He took a towel in hand and began to wash the feet of His disciples. When He had finished washing from their feet the last coat of dust and camel dung from the streets of downtown Jerusalem, He made it very clear what the stakes of obedience are:

"You call me 'Teacher' and 'Lord' and rightly so, for that is what I am. Now that I, your Lord and Teacher, have washed your feet, you also should wash one another's feet. I have set you an example that you should do as I have done for you. . . . A new command I give you: Love one another. As I have loved you, so you must love one another. By this all men will know that you are my disciples, if you love one another" (John 13:13-15, 34-35).

GOING TO EXTREMES

Your mission with this curriculum on "Extreme Friendship" is to help students count the cost of that kind of authentic love. "Extreme Friendship" is designed to help you and your students explore the challenges, difficulties, and practical realities of loving as Jesus loved, and learn what it really means to be friends ". . . if the Lord's the Lord of them" ("Friends," Michael W. Smith).

Why is this so hard? What is it about who we are and the culture in which we live that makes Extreme Friendship so extremely tough? No doubt, there are lots of factors that make intimacy and genuine friendship such a stranger to us, but let me suggest three that are especially at work in the world of your junior high students.

- ***They don't know what friendship means.*** Your junior highers are growing up in a world in which commitment has been drained of any real meaning. Marriage vows that promised to love and cherish "til death do us part" are bulldozed out of the way because the promise-makers decided "it just wasn't working out." Professional athletes switch teams at the drop of a hat, or more accurately, at the drop of a larger pay check. The old concept of a neighborhood as a place of community and shared responsibility has been replaced by a sterile geographical term describing the temporary stopping place of families on the move who occupy a certain property until the next transfer comes along. In short, commitment means, "I am committed to you until I am no longer committed to you."

  It's in this cold, arid relational climate that kids are trying to forge friendships and understand commitment. No wonder that most kids define friendship in terms of what another person will do for them: "A friend is someone who will lie for you (when you need an alibi), buy for you (if you're underage), and pry for you (when you want to find out if he/she will go out with you)." The "towel concept" seems kind of extreme in that culture.

- ***They don't know what friendship looks like.*** Remember, these are kids who have learned about friendship by watching a TV show called "Friends" where several incredibly beautiful people work through all kinds of problems in just under 30 minutes—with non-stop laughs in the process! Even when they tune into MTV to see the "Real World," where they get to watch real people who live real lives wrestle with real issues, it probably doesn't dawn on them that the entire premise of the show is completely unreal. How many teenagers and 20-somethings do you know who are given $50,000 by some TV producers to start their own business, and offered a fully furnished waterfront home in Miami while they work through "real life" worries?

  The good news is the gallery is not bare. God has given us a number of vivid, deeply touching portraits of true friendship in His Word. There is Nathan, the friend who cared enough to confront David (2 Samuel 12). And Aquila and Priscilla, the fabric merchants from Corinth, who probably offered financial support to their friend Paul the Apostle and traveled with him on his missionary journey to Ephesus (Acts 18:18). Or what about Barnabas, the "Son of Encouragement," always ready with an act of kindness, who was committed enough to his young friend John Mark not to give up on him when others did (Acts 15:36ff)? And who could not be moved by the tapestry of David and Jonathan, two men whose lives are interwoven in remarkable and even tragic ways? Of course, Jesus is the ultimate model God has given us to show what friendship looks like.

And that's what this book is all about. It asks the critical question, "What kind of friend would Jesus be?"

Many junior highers believe that Jesus was a really nice guy who walked around telling people "It'll be all right" and "I'll be there for you." The truth is, Jesus was an Extreme Friend. He wasn't just nice. He put friendship into action.

You'll find quickly that none of the lessons in this book are "new." Service. Encouragement. Forgiveness. Accountability. Introducing our friends to Jesus. They don't represent some trendy new twist on friendship. They are foundational lessons that teach the basic friendship skills most junior highers still need to master. When junior highers meet a God who serves them, who forgives them, and who believes in them, they'll meet a mind-blowing God. They will certainly become better friends to each other when they build their own friendship with Jesus.

They don't know how friendship works. One of the especially helpful aspects of this curriculum is that it encourages students to take those baby steps of practical obedience. It is not enough to walk wide-mouthed and open-eyed through the gallery of biblical friendship. God calls us to take up the brush and begin to paint these relationships into our own lives. That means we must emphasize the "how-to" of friendship.

Duffy Robbins is Chairman of the Department of Youth Ministry at Eastern College in St. Davids, Pennsylvania. He is also a well-known conference speaker, seminar leader, and author.

SESSION 1

Extreme Friends

YOUR GOALS FOR THIS SESSION:

Choose one or more

- [ ] To help students get an overview of what kind of friend Jesus was on earth—He put friendship into action.
- [ ] To help students understand a mind-blowing idea about service: Jesus served others instead of demanding to be served.
- [ ] To challenge students to be Extreme Friends—friends who put friendship into action by serving others like Jesus did.
- [ ] Other: ____

____

Your Bible Base

Mark 6:30-44
Mark 7:31-37
Luke 6:17-26
Luke 10:25-37
Luke 10:38-42
John 11:1-44

STEP 1

Name that Foot

OPTIONS

Below, students try to guess the identity of six mystery feet: 5-10 minutes. Or, choose an option category from the sidebar and see pages 23-27 for more "Getting Together" options.

Supplies needed: posterboard and tape (or window curtains, mural paper, or chalkboard on wheels and bedding sheets), paper, pencils, CD player and CD (or other way to play music).
Set up: Make a large "mystery curtain" (about 8' x 5') by taping posterboard together or use other supplies listed above. Recruit adult or student volunteers to hold the curtain in place between the doorway to your room and the place where your group will sit. Pass out paper and pencils.

Choose six volunteers to be "mystery guests." Escort them out of the room and tell them to take their shoes and socks off. Have them re-enter the room completely hidden from the rest of the group by the mystery curtain—except for their bare feet. The rest of the group members write down their guesses as to which foot belongs to which mystery student. Consider having upbeat music playing in the background. Anyone who correctly guesses the identity of all six feet earns a dirty sock as a prize. That's nothing to sniff at! If you have time, repeat the game with six more mystery guests.

A good way to transition from a fun activity to the heart of the lesson is to throw out a "quick question" students can discuss with one or two people next to them. Ask: **In this game, we found out how well you know each other—well, at least how well you know each other's big toes. Do you think knowing someone well is *the* key to having a good friendship? If not, what *do* you think is the key to a good friendship?**

STEP 2

Friendship Collages

Below, students clip words and pictures out of newspapers and magazines to make collages that reflect "great" friendships: 10-15 minutes.
Or, choose an option category from the sidebar and see pages 23-27 for more "Getting Thirsty" options.

Supplies needed: old magazines, newspapers, scissors, glue, markers, posterboard, tape.
Set up: Divide into small teams (optimal size four to six students) and give each team a piece of posterboard and other collage supplies.

Discuss: **What kinds of things do you do with your friends? What makes your friendships "great"?** Explain that instead of just talking about their friendships, your students will have a chance to *show* what their friendships are all about. Give them 10 minutes to cut out and paste together as many words, pictures, and symbols they can find that show: 1) what kinds of things they do with their friends, and 2) what makes their friendships great. Then let one person from each team explain the collages. Tape all the collages to a wall in your room. You will refer to them in Step 3.

How many of you are satisfied with mediocre or just OK friendships? How many of you want friendships that are "great" like the ones described by your collages?

If you really want great friendships, where do go to learn more about great friendship? Who do you look to as a model of great friendship?

If you really want great friendships in your life, you'll study the greatest friend of all time. And that's exactly what we're going to do in this series. Jesus Christ is the world's all-time greatest friend. He can teach us some mind-blowing things about friendship. He can show us how to go beyond mediocre, OK friendship so we can build Extreme Friendships.

Teacher Tip: Making collages can be a successful activity for many junior high groups if you keep a couple things in mind: First, be sure to provide magazines that students will enjoy thumbing through (like *Sports Illustrated* for guys and *Brio* or similar magazines for girls). Add a competition element. For example, you might throw out the challenge: **Who can fill up their posterboard with the most pictures?** Finally, give each team a small enough piece of posterboard that it's a realistic goal to cover up all the empty space in the time allotted.

OPTIONS

STEP 3

Jesus Collages

Below, students make collages that reflect Jesus' friendships: 15-20 minutes. Or, choose an option category from the sidebar and see pages 23-27 for more "Getting the Word" options.

OPTIONS

Supplies needed: Bibles, collage supplies (from Step 2), white board, marker.
Set up: List the following Bible passages on white board ahead of time: Mark 6:30-44; Mark 7:31-37; Luke 6:17-26; Luke 10:38-42; and John 11:1-44. These are the passages students will study to get an overview of the kind of friend Jesus was. Pass out new sheets of posterboard. If students need to replenish their supply of collage materials (magazines, newspapers, markers, scissors, glue) pass these supplies out, too.

Have students stay in the small groups from Step 2. Ask each group to use a Bible to read the verses you've listed on the board and answer two questions for each verse: 1) What words best describe the kind of friend Jesus was? and 2) What pictures come to mind when you think of how Jesus treated others? Each group should make a second collage based on their answers by writing down words, drawing pictures, or clipping words and pictures out of magazines and newspapers. Give students 10 minutes to complete the new collages.

Hang the new "Jesus collages" on a wall next to the "friendship collages" students made in Step 2. Discuss:

What kinds of words and pictures did you use to describe Jesus' friendship with others? Why?

What *kind* of people did Jesus befriend?

Did Jesus just talk about being a great friend to people in need? Or did He put His friendship into action? How did He put His friendship into action? Supplement students' answers by saying something like: **Jesus was an Extreme Friend—He didn't just say "I'll be there for you." He wasn't just "nice" to His friends. He put His friendship into action by SERVING others.**

If Jesus was an Extreme Friend, what kind of friends do you think we should be?

STEP 4

How to be an Extreme Friend

Below, students use Resource 1 to brainstorm ideas about how to be Extreme Friends in various real-world situations: 10-15 minutes. Or, choose an option category from the sidebar and see pages 23-27 for more "Getting the Point" options.

Supplies needed: cut-out copies of Resource 1, "What's a Friend to Do?" (page 21), paper, pens.
Set up: Ahead of time, cut a copy of Resource 1 into five pieces along the dotted lines. (If you have more than 30 students, you will need to cut apart more than one copy of Resource 1.)

Introduce the parable of the Good Samaritan by saying something like: **Jesus told a story that can help us apply the extreme idea about service in the real world.**

As a group, read Luke 10:25-37. If your students have trouble relating to the context of the story, you might also try reading this modern paraphrase:

A man was hitchhiking from Chicago to Detroit when some guys jumped him, stole his wallet, beat him up, and left him lying by the side of the road. A pastor drove by and saw him, but the pastor was busy rehearsing his sermon and kept on going. Then a businesswoman drove by, but she was late for a meeting and quickly changed lanes to pass him. Finally, a beat up Chevy pulled to a stop. A poorly dressed man with dirty fingernails, messy hair, and an odd smell got out and put the man in his car. He took him to the nearby Hilton, ordered room service, and made sure the hotel doctor took care of him. The man spent every dime he had to take care of the stranger.

How does this modern paraphrase help you better understand the story of the Good Samaritan?

What do you think Jesus wants us to learn from the story of the Good Samaritan?

What does this story teach us about being Extreme Friends?

Supplement students' answers with the following info as needed: **Unlike the two other people in the story, the Good Samaritan saw someone in need and he said, "Whatever it takes, I'm going to put this person first and serve him." He was an**

O P T I O N S

Extreme Friend because He served others just like Jesus did.

Form small groups of four to six students. Give each group one of the cut-out pieces of Resource 1, a blank sheet of paper, and pens. Ask each group to look at its card from the resource sheet and think about this question: **What would it look like to be an Extreme Friend in this situation?** Tell the groups to write down as many ways they can think of to serve someone in that scenario. After five or six minutes ask each group to read its final list out loud. Write down all the ideas on a white board. Make sure to congratulate your students on the creativity of ideas they have shared.

Say something like: **Now we have a clear picture of what it would look like to be Extreme Friends in the real world. You can see that none of these ideas is easy, but they're all worth it. Are you up for the challenge? Will you choose to be an Extreme Friend?**

BIBLE BYTES

The Good Samaritan

Luke 10:25-37

◆ BACKGROUND BYTES: Most Jewish leaders regarded the Samaritans unclean and chose not to associate with them. Jews resented the fact that many Samaritans had intermarried with the unbelieving Moabites, which the Jews thought corrupted their Jewish faith. The feud got so heated that sometime around Jesus' birth, a group of Samaritans had scattered bones in the Jewish temple at Passover.

◆ SCRIPTURE BYTES: Religious leaders were familiar with the teaching in Leviticus 19:18 to "love your neighbor," but they had made up a number of rules about who their neighbors were. Jesus taught that following God involved radical love for all people, especially those in need. For more on what Jesus taught about love, see: Matthew 5:38-48; Matthew 25:31-46; and John 15:9-15.

◆ BYTE-SIZE INSIGHTS: The Good Samaritan's love for the injured man is a model of the way Jesus loves us as sinners: Jesus sought out those who needed Him and gave everything He had to help them, to the point of dying for them on the cross. • Jesus gives us the power to love and serve others when we ask. Students who don't have an empowering relationship with Jesus Christ will find loving and serving others a nearly impossible struggle, no matter how hard they try.

STEP 5

Putting Service into Action

Below, students look for opportunities to be Extreme Friends outside the meeting place, then sign their initials to one service idea: 10-15 minutes. Or, choose an option category from the sidebar and see pages 23-27 for more "Getting Personal" options.

Supplies needed: list of "Extreme Friendship" ideas from Step 4, pens, transportation (optional).

Let's not just talk about being Extreme Friends. Let's get out and do it. Explain that students have 10 minutes to walk around with a partner and look for ways to be an Extreme Friend somewhere right outside your meeting place. Give them a few ideas, such as being an Extreme Friend to the gardener by pulling weeds in specific places around the church, or to the custodian by picking up some trash, or to a single parent trying to walk his or her children to their Sunday school class.

When students return, discuss: **How did you put friendship into action? How did it feel?**

It's usually easier to be Extreme Friends here at church rather than out in the real world but let's think about the rest of the week. Of all of the ideas we listed earlier, which idea sticks out to you as the best way you can put friendship into action this next week?

Explain that if students would like to commit to putting service into action this week by doing one of the ideas on the list on the board made in Step 4, they should come forward and put their initials next to that idea. If a student has another idea that hasn't been mentioned yet, he or she can write that idea down, then put his or her own initials next to it. Give your students a few minutes to complete this task. You may want to lead the way by placing your own initials next to an idea.

After your students have finished, close in prayer. Pray that God will strengthen each person to be an Extreme Friend this week.

Teacher Tip: The "Service Tour" directions above work best for Sunday school classes. But if you're meeting at another time or place, you can modify the directions as needed. Or you might arrange some kind of service opportunity your group can do right where you are. For example, you might cook a meal for a needy family (give small groups of students responsibility for preparing different parts of the meal). Consider your time and other limitations and be creative!

OPTIONS

SMALL GROUP

FELLOWSHIP & WORSHIP

SHORT MEETING TIME

What's a Friend to Do?

WHAT YOU SAY
IN CLASS TO A FRIEND

WHAT YOU SAY
AFTER SCHOOL TO A FRIEND

WHAT YOU DO
WITH A FRIEND
ON THE WEEKEND

WHAT YOU DO
WITH A FRIEND WHEN
YOU'RE AT HER OR HIS HOME

WHAT YOU DO
WITH A FRIEND DURING
LUNCH AT SCHOOL

EXTRA ACTION

STEP 1 - EXTREME CLAYMATION

Play a variation of "Win, Lose, or Draw" using modeling clay.

To introduce the concept of Extreme Friendship, put the following words on slips of paper: bungee jumping, mountain biking, snowboarding, rock climbing, friendship. Divide into teams of four to six students and give each team modeling clay or dough. Each team should choose a "modeler." Pick the first clue and show it to each modeler. The team that first shouts out the clue being modeled wins one point. (No words or gestures allowed.) Discuss: **What did all of the clues have in common?** (They are "extreme" activities.) **Do you think "friendship" belongs with the rest of the clues? Why or why not? When is friendship "extreme"?** Say: **Extreme Friendship is being a friend like Jesus. Jesus is the ultimate modeler of Extreme Friendship. He always lived on the edge and pushed the status quo. What kind of friendship do you model?** *(Needed: modeling clay or play dough, slips of paper, pen or pencil.)*

STEP 4 - WILD BALL BRAINSTORM

Play a game with tennis balls to help students brainstorm serving ideas.

After discussing the parable of the Good Samaritan, use this activity to add more action to the brainstorming of service ideas: Divide into equal teams of four to six. Have teams circle up; give each team a tennis ball. Read the first scenario on Resource 1. When you say go, one person on each team names one way he or she can put friendship into action in that scenario. That student throws the ball to another in the circle, who names a different answer, and so on. See how fast teams can get. Repeat with as many scenarios as you have time for. *(Needed: copies of Resource 1, tennis balls.)*

SMALL GROUP

STEP 1 - TWO TRUTHS & A LIE

Guess which of three statements is a lie.

"Name that Foot" requires six mystery guests. Instead, have students tell two true and one false statements about themselves. Others must guess which is the lie.

STEPS 2/3 - HUMAN COLLAGES

Make "human friendship collages."

In a small group, making collages may not produce enough ideas for an effective discussion. Instead, bring in a wide variety of odd and normal objects to represent different aspects of friendship. As a group, make a human collage representing a "good friend" by posing, adding props, and making up additional signs and symbols to place on one volunteer. Be creative—a wrench in his hand might represent that a good friend "fixes" problems; a ring on his finger might represent that a good friend is committed. After reading the Scripture passages, make a second human collage to represent the kind of friend Jesus was. You might include props like: a hammer (He built into His friends), torn clothes (He made Himself a lowly servant), a wooden cross (to represent His death). *(Needed: various objects.)*

STEP 5 - SERVICE PROJECT

Drive to or plan a service project.

Instead of using the service tour idea, you have a great opportunity with a small group to arrange a service project ahead of time. You might arrange to drive your students off-site and serve in a soup kitchen or help with a project like Habitat for Humanity. The best projects will involve enough sacrifice to challenge students and enough service for them to experience some of the rewards of befriending and serving people in need. If you can't arrange the project ahead of time, you might spend a few minutes planning a project for a different meeting time. *(Needed: variable.)*

LARGE GROUP

STEP 1 - NAME THAT CHANGE

Identify changes in a partner.

In a large group, your students may not even know each other's names, much less their feet! Instead of playing "Name that Foot," have your students pair up with and face one friend. They should take a minute to notice their partner's hair, clothes, and other physical characteristics. Then pairs should stand back to back and students should change three things about themselves (unbutton a button, tousle their hair, untie a shoe, and so on). Finally, have the pairs face each other again and try to identify the changes.

STEPS 2/3 - WORD STORMS

Instead of making collages of pictures, brainstorm word collages.

The collages described in Steps 2 and 3 could be difficult for large groups—we're talking a lot of magazines and glue! Instead, divide into groups of six to eight and have each group brainstorm a list of words and phrases. Write these down on posterboard or newsprint in lieu of magazine pictures. In Step 2, the words should describe students' friendships. In Step 3, the words should describe Jesus' friendships. You might make it a contest each time to see which group can create the longest list or the list that contains the most ideas not found on other groups' lists. *(Needed: pens or markers, newsprint or posterboard.)*

Step 3 - Sloppy Skits

Add impromptu skits that answer: What if Jesus practiced "sloppy agape"?

Many well-meaning church groups practice "sloppy agape"—they put too much emphasis on being "nice" but they don't put friendship into action. If this is reflected in your students' collages from Step 2, point it out. Discuss: **Friends say stuff like "I'll be there for you" and "It'll be alright" all the time. What do those phrases mean?** If students are honest they may admit those phrases are just "nice" things friends say but don't often relate to action. Instead of making more collages, have each group perform a skit that shows what its Scripture passage might have looked like if Jesus was just "nice." For example, the Mark 6:30-44 group might show Jesus, instead of feeding the crowd, simply saying, "I'm sorry you're hungry. But it's OK. I'm here for you." After each presentation, read what Jesus really did. Brainstorm words to define Extreme Friendship (sacrifice, service, etc.).

Step 4 - Friendship Interview

Interview two Extreme Friends.

Even groups that have "heard it all" will probably still respond to seeing it in action. Invite two old and "extreme" friends to tell stories to your group. Encourage the friends to talk honestly and openly. As they talk about a difficult friendship issue, it will wake up kids to listen closely. Some potential follow-up questions include: **What's the most you ever sacrificed for your friend? Have there been any tough times? How did your friendship survive? How hard was it to forgive?** *(Needed: two guest interviewees.)*

Step 2 - Ideal Collages

Make collages that reflect what should *be.*

Rather than making collages that describe students' actual friendships, make collages that show what friendship *should* be. Ask students to think about: **What are the qualities you look for in a friend?** This variation will better prepare students with little Bible background to see that Jesus is the ideal friend they are looking for. *(Needed: collage supplies from Step 2.)*

Step 3 - Friend for Today

Tell how Jesus is a friend to you today.

Help students understand Jesus wasn't just a great friend a long time ago—He is a great friend today. Follow the directions for Step 3, then discuss: **How can Jesus provide for our needs today? In what ways can Jesus heal us? How does Jesus serve us? How does He comfort us?** Be prepared to discuss specific experiences of your own. For example, try not to just say, "Jesus answered my prayers"; give details like "I was praying for a way to pay my rent and I got an unexpected refund check in the mail."

Step 4 - Extreme Testimonies

Guest speakers tell how Extreme Friendship is our response to Jesus.

Students with little Bible background may need help making the jump from "Jesus is a good friend" to "We should be good friends like Jesus." Recruit spiritually mature high school students or adults to give one- or two-minute testimonies about why and how they try to be good friends to others because Jesus is such a good friend to them. They should detail their motives (thankfulness to Jesus, wanting to obey Scripture, etc.) and the specific ways they try to be Extreme Friends. Once you've made this introduction, use Step 4 as directed. *(Needed: guest speakers.)*

Step 3 - Celebrate Jesus

Spend extra time worshiping Jesus for the friend He is to us.

After completing Step 3, you might use one or more of these ideas to help students reflect on and praise Jesus for the friend He is to us:

- Write thank You letters to Jesus.
- Read John 13:1-9. Discuss that this was one more story of Jesus putting friendship into action with service, and wash each student's feet with water and a wash rag.
- Read "The Ragman" by Walter Wangerin, Jr. (*Ragman and Other Cries of Faith*, Harper & Row, 1984) or another story that helps illuminate the extreme idea that Jesus serves us.
- Sing worship songs you are familiar with that celebrate Jesus' friendship with us or His servant's attitude toward us.

(Needed: pens, paper, Bibles, bucket of water, wash rag, story,or *worship music.)*

Step 5 - Power Prayers

Pray for God's power to help put friendship into action.

This idea for an extended prayer time will help students close the meeting with an upward focus. Divide into groups of three. Help students get in a quiet mood by turning the lights down and singing several praise songs. As you finish singing, ask students to close their eyes. Read Proverbs 17:17a to them: "A friend loves at all times . . . ." If you want, challenge students to memorize the verse. Then ask students to take a minute and pray for the others in their group. Students should pray that God will give them courage and opportunities to put specific friendship ideas into action. *(Needed: Bibles, worship music.)*

MOSTLY GIRLS

STEP 1 - NAME THAT BABY FACE

Identify mystery baby pictures.

Girls love looking at things that identify themselves and their friends. Identifying baby pictures might be more fun for a group of mostly girls than the "Name that Foot" game. Tell students ahead of time to bring their baby pictures in. Mix up the baby pictures and tape them to a large piece of cardboard or to a wall. Assign each photo a number. Distribute index cards and ask students to list the number of each photo on their card followed by the name of the girl they believe each photo shows. Reveal the true identities and see who got the most answers right. Discuss: **What similarities do you see in the baby photos and in each other as you are now?** Say: **Every one of you has a Friend who not only knows exactly what you looked like as a baby, He actually knew you before you were born! Jesus knows you inside and out. You may know that He wants to be your best friend. In this series we'll also learn He wants to teach you how to be good friends to others.** *(Needed: baby photos, tape, cardboard, index cards, pens.)*

STEP 2 - INDIVIDUAL COLLAGES

Make personal collages as gifts for friends.

Friendship is a strong value for many girls; a value they love to share and celebrate. Follow the directions for Step 2 with this variation: Have each girl make her own friendship collage as a gift she can give later to one of her friends. Pass out a small piece of posterboard to each student. Put collage supplies in a place where students can share. Tell girls to cut and paste words, pictures, and symbols that represent the specific friendship they choose. Give each student a chance to display her collage. Use the concluding comments as written in Step 2. *(Needed: collage supplies from Step 2.)*

MOSTLY GUYS

STEP 1 - X-TREME GAMES

Use activities with an "extreme" theme.

Guys will eat up any tie-in you can make to "extreme" activities before talking about Extreme Friendship. Consider these ideas:

- **Extreme Video:** Watch a clip from an extreme sports video (e.g., *Angel's Cliff* or any other video by Warren Miller).
- **Extreme Diving**: Lay a couple of gym mats or mattresses down. See who can make the most "extreme" dive.
- **Extreme Athlete Contest:** Decide who the "Most Extreme Athlete" is by holding a combination of contests, including pushups, foot races, weightlifting, etc. *(Needed: variable.)*

STEPS 2/3 - ULTIMATE POSTERS

Design posters of The Extreme Guy.

Instead of asking students to make collages of their friendships, ask them to design the "Ultimate Guy" or "Most Extreme Guy" posters. Discuss: **How does the Ultimate Guy treat his friends? Is it "extreme" or "uncool" to serve others? Why? What would happen if you sacrificed for and served your friends?** Then follow Step 3 as directed and compare the Ultimate Guy posters to the Jesus collages. Ask guys if they want to change any part of their posters to reflect the kind of Ultimate Guy Jesus is. *(Needed: collage supplies from Step 2.)*

STEPS 4/5 - 6:2 CHALLENGE

Challenge guys to carry rocks up a hill.

Find a challenging hill to climb or trail to hike and take your group there. Make each student start the hike carrying something heavy, like a huge rock. When the guys get tired, take as many of their rocks as possible and carry them up the rest of the way. At the end of the trail explain that's what Extreme Friendship is—it's not just saying nice things, it's jumping in and sacrificing so your friend is better off. Challenge students to read and memorize Galatians 6:2. *(Needed: rocks.)*

EXTRA FUN

STEP 1 - FRIENDSHIP PARTY

Introduce the friendship series with a variety of games and fun activities.

Consider these ideas:

- **Famous Friends:** Have teams list pairs of famous friends—real or fictitious. Award prizes to the team with the most.
- **Do I Know You?:** This is kind of a "Newlywed Game" for friends. Have kids pair up, then send one half of every pair out of the room. Ask questions of the remaining friends. Then bring the others back in and check answers.
- **Draw a Friend:** Give groups of four large sheets of butcher paper and markers. Have them draw a life-sized "perfect friend."
- **Friendship Food:** Serve snacks (candy, cookies, chips, etc.) Have kids choose a snack item, hold it up, and describe why that item is like friendship (e.g., "This cookie is like friendship because going through heat made it better"). *(Needed: variable.)*

STEPS 2/3 - PROP COMMERCIALS

Teams create commercials for friendship using assigned props.

Divide into about four teams (optimal size: four or five students each). Display a collection of odd props, like: a toilet plunger, a stapler, a Frisbee, a box, a radio, a rope, and a teddy bear. Be creative and choose an odd assortment. Explain to the teams that they'll have five minutes to create a commercial that reflects what a good friendship is like. The only rules are that it has to be 30 seconds or less, has to be about friendship, and must use all the props. (The props can be used to *represent* something else, however.) After several minutes, have the teams perform their commercials. Repeat this activity for Step 3, asking the teams to put together commercials that reflect the friendship characteristics of Jesus. *(Needed: various odd props.)*

MEDIA

STEP 1 - REAL WORLD VIDEO
Show short clips of students' bedrooms.

Make arrangements ahead of time with a parent to film a student's room but don't let the student know, but keep the segment short. Record clips of you being greeted by a parent, pictures of the student on the wall, and an in-depth look at various parts of the student's room. Cue the video and say: **How well do we really know our friends? Let's take take an in-depth look at one student's private world. See if anything surprises you about how [he or she] *really* lives.** For an ongoing gag, film a different student's room each week. *(Needed: TV, VCR, video camera.)*

STEP 2 - MEDIA AND THE MESSAGE
Listen to songs with "friends" themes.

Arrange for students to bring in songs that contain messages about friendship. Even secular music can help you contrast Jesus' ideas about friendship with the world's. Give each student a chance play part of the song, explain what the message about friendship is, and tell what they like or dislike about the message. Be prepared to point out any differences from Jesus' views on friendships. *(Needed: songs students bring in, CD player and/or cassette player.)*

SHORT MEETING TIME

STEP 1 - FRIENDSHIP STORIES
Tell a partner about a good friend.

Instead of waiting for all students to arrive, as students enter have them pair up and tell each other about one important friend. (Also, remember that if you're *really* short on time and your group doesn't need to be "warmed up," you can always skip Step 1 altogether without missing any of the "meat" of the lesson.)

STEP 2 - PHOTO COLLAGES
Use students' own photos for a collage.

Prepare students ahead of time to bring in photos of themselves with their friends in a variety of activities. Instead of having students take the time to cut pictures out of magazines, make one "friendship collage" using the pictures students brought in. Modify the discussion in Step 2 as needed. *(Needed: students' photos, posterboard, tape.)*

STEP 3 - MINI MELODRAMAS
Pantomime Scripture stories.

Instead of making "Jesus collages," read each Bible story one at a time. Have volunteers act out the actions of their assigned characters. Then compare Jesus' friendships to students' friendships as directed in Step 3. *(Needed: Bibles.)*

STEP 4 - ONE MASTER LIST
Instead of using Resource 1, make one list.

Brainstorm one list of ways students can serve others. *(Needed: newsprint, marker.)*

STEP 5 - SKIP THE TOUR
Decorate collages made in Step 2.

Skip the tour around the church. Return to the collages or posters made in Step 2. Let students decorate the old collages by drawing new pictures with markers or crayons that symbolize what they will do to serve others in the coming week. *(Needed: collages from Step 2.)*

URBAN

STEP 1 - NAME THAT NOSE
Identify mystery noses.

If your group members find exposing their feet awkward, modify the Name that Foot directions slightly: Cut a space in the mystery curtain for noses and have the group guess who those belong to. (This also works with thumbs and mouths!) *(Needed: mystery curtain from Step 1.)*

STEPS 2/3 - URBAN COLLAGES
Use urban magazines for the collages.

To make the friendship collage applicable to the cultural images experienced by city teens, bring in magazines like: *Emerge, Right On, Vibe, Bronze Thrills, Braids and Beauty, Ebony, Essence, Black Enterprise, Jive, The Source, Jet, Hype Hair, YSB, Free 4080, Upscale, Black Hair, Heart & Soul, Black Beat,* and any others you know of. *(Needed: collage supplies from Step 2 and above.)*

STEP 4 - THE URBAN SAMARITAN
Read an urban paraphrase of the parable.

Instead of the paraphrase included in the main lesson, read this urban version of Luke 10:25-37: Two days before Christmas, Hector Fernandez missed the last bus home by seconds and had to walk 10 miles. He was stopped by three gang members who accused him of being on the wrong side of town, beat him, and left him there bleeding. They also took all his cash—the Christmas bonus Hector needed to buy gifts for his family. A pastor looking to help the homeless drove by. "Hello, do you need a sandwich or a cup of coffee?" Hector said, "I'm hurt! I need an ambulance!" But the pastor just threw him a sandwich and drove on. Next a jogger ran by. Hector tried to motion that he was hurt. The jogger, startled, crossed the street and kept going. Finally, a police car pulled up. This officer attended to Hector, took him immediately to the best hospital in town, paid the hospital bill at his own expense, and raised enough money to buy gifts for all Hector's family for Christmas.

Steps 2/3 - Friendship Box

Pick items out of a box and give two-to five-sentence "friendship messages."

If some of the high school students in your group would find the collage activities "cheesy," try this creative discussion starter. Fill up a "Friendship Box" with random items, some that have to do with friendship (friendship bracelet, phone, pictures of friends, etc.) and some where the connection is not so obvious (toilet plunger, lava lamp, baseball, anything else wacky enough to get your students' attention). Each student or pair of students must choose an item from the box and give a two- to five-sentence mini-message on friendship based on that item. For example, a student might pick the phone and give a message about how good communication is an important part of friendship. For Step 3, students should use the same objects to give mini-messages about what Jesus thinks about friendship. *(Needed: box, various odd items.)*

Step 4 - Extreme News

Write newspaper accounts of what might happen if students acted like Jesus.

This activity might work better with high schoolers in the group because their answers will help inspire your junior highers. Divide into groups of four or five, each a mixture of some junior and senior high students. Tell students to imagine what kinds of headlines and newspaper stories might be written about their group if they were to become Extreme Friends like Jesus. They might come up with headlines like "Youth Group Impacts Campus" and specific stories about how teens serve others at their school by providing for those who have needs for food or clothes, spending time with less popular students, etc. Pass out a large sheet of newsprint and markers for each group to record its answers and share them with the rest of the group. *(Needed: newsprint, markers.)*

Step 2 - Memory Game

Play a memory game that involves describing terrible and ideal friends.

Sixth graders are concrete thinkers. This memory game is a fun, concrete way to begin defining friendship. Sit in a circle (or divide into circles of 10-15 students each if you have a large group). For the first round, start the game by saying, "An ideal friend is . . . thoughtful." Point to your head. As you continue to your left, each player then repeats the words and actions of those before them and then adds a new word and a new action. This continues until all but one player has made a mistake and dropped out of the game. Before moving on, make a list of all the words or phrases players used to describe an ideal friend. Record these on newsprint or white board. If you have time, start another round with "A terrible friend is. . . ." *(Needed: newsprint or white board, marker.)*

Step 3 - Word Race

Teams race to find four words to describe how Jesus treated His friends.

Write the following headings on newsprint or white board: "Normal" and "Extreme." Divide into five teams and give each team a pen and paper. Assign each team one of the five Scripture passages listed on page 17. Teams should write down four words to describe how Jesus treated His friends in their passage. Discuss: **How did Jesus treat His friends? Was he just a normal friend or did He ever do anything extreme?** Have students list their four words under either the "Normal" or "Extreme" headings. Most words, like serving, helping, and caring, belong under "Extreme." *(Needed: Bibles, pens, paper, newsprint or white board, marker.)*

Planning Checklist

Step 1 (5-10 minutes, unless noted)

- ❑ **Extra Action:** Extreme Claymation
- ❑ **Small Group:** Two Truths & A Lie
- ❑ **Large Group:** Name that Change
- ❑ **Mostly Girls:** Name that Baby Face
- ❑ **Mostly Guys:** X-treme Games
- ❑ **Extra Fun:** Friendship Party (15 min.)
- ❑ **Media:** Real World Video
- ❑ **Short Time:** Friendship Stories (3-5 min.)
- ❑ **Urban:** Name that Nose

Step 2 (10-15 minutes, unless noted)

- ❑ **Small Group:** Human Collages*
- ❑ **Large Group:** Word Storms*
- ❑ **Little Bible:** Ideal Collages (30 min.)
- ❑ **Mostly Girls:** Individ. Collages (30 min.)
- ❑ **Mostly Guys:** Ultimate Posters (30 min.)*
- ❑ **Extra Fun:** Prop Commercials (30 min.)*
- ❑ **Media:** Media and the Message
- ❑ **Short Time:** Photo Collages (5-10 min.)
- ❑ **Urban:** Urban Collages (30 min.)*
- ❑ **Combined:** Friendship Box (30 min.)*
- ❑ **Sixth Grade:** Memory Game

Step 3 (15-20 minutes, unless noted)

- ❑ **Heard It All:** Sloppy Skits
- ❑ **Little Bible:** Friend for Today
- ❑ **Fellowship & Worship:** Celebrate Jesus
- ❑ **Short Time:** Mini Melodramas (30 min.)*
- ❑ **Sixth Grade:** Word Race

Step 4 (10-15 minutes, unless noted)

- ❑ **Extra Action:** Wild Ball Brainstorm
- ❑ **Heard It All:** Friendship Interview
- ❑ **Little Bible:** Extreme Testimonies
- ❑ **Mostly Guys:** 6:2 Challenge (30 min.)*
- ❑ **Short Time:** One Master List (30 min.)*
- ❑ **Urban:** The Urban Samaritan
- ❑ **Combined:** Extreme News

Step 5 (5-10 minutes, unless noted)

- ❑ **Small Group:** Service Project
- ❑ **Fellowship & Worship:** Power Prayers
- ❑ **Short Time:** Skip the Tour (5 min.)

** two combined steps*

SESSION 2

Bleacher Friends

YOUR GOALS FOR THIS SESSION:

Choose one or more

- ☐ To help students learn how Jesus valued a bleeding woman others labeled "unvaluable."
- ☐ To help students discover a mind-blowing truth about value: In Jesus' eyes, even the unvalued are invaluable.
- ☐ To help students become Bleacher Friends—friends who "cheer on" and value people like Jesus did.
- ☐ Other: ______________________________

Your Bible Base

Mark 5:21-34

STEP 1

Marshmallow Mash

Below, students play a wild, crazy marshmallow game that teases the topic of value and worth: 5-10 minutes.
Or, choose one of the option categories in the sidebar and see pages 39-43 for more "Getting Together" options.

Supplies needed: several bags of large marshmallows; rope, tape, or cones.
Set up: Divide your room into four equal areas using tape, rope, or cones. It would be helpful but not necessary to move chairs and tables out of the way. Then divide your group into four teams. For best results, divide according to natural affinity groups, such as school, gender, or grade level. Assign each team one of the four areas.

When you say go, have teams try to throw any marshmallows out of their team area and into another team's area. When you call stop, the team with the least marshmallows in its area wins. Make a big deal of congratulating the members of the winning team. Treat them like they're more important than members of the losing team.

Have students discuss the following questions with one or two people next to them: **Do you think winners are more valuable than losers? Why or why not? If not, why is winning such a big deal? And why is it that one of the worst things you can call somebody is a "loser"?**

Teacher Tip: Many competitive junior high students will still fall for the age-old trick of making a contest out of cleaning up. If your group will go for it, challenge teams to see which can pick up all of its marshmallows first. For added fun, tell students they can only use their feet.

OPTIONS

STEP 2

The Price Is Right

Below, students play a version of the "The Price Is Right" game show and discuss the Value Trap: 10-15 minutes.
Or, choose one of the option categories in the sidebar and see pages 39-43 for more "Getting Thirsty" options.

Supplies needed: pen and paper, Post-It notes (substitute cardboard or posterboard, scissors and tape), marker, magazine pictures of both current celebrities and people considered "outcasts," and approximately seven household and food items, such as garbage bags, laundry detergent, candles, cookies, cake mix, etc.
Set up: Ahead of time, remove the price tags from each household and food item, but keep a list of the correct prices. For each item, make a new price tag that is 10 cents either higher or lower than the actual price. Price tags can be as simple as a Post-It note, or more elaborate tags cut out of cardboard or posterboard. Use a marker to write the new price on the price tag. For the second part of this activity you'll need to clip a handful of pictures of celebrities out of magazines. Try to choose some that are popular with your group and others that are in the "out" crowd. Also clip out pictures of "unvalued" people: the homeless, elderly, poor, etc.

Introduce the game by saying something like: **How many of you have seen "The Price is Right" game show? Who wants to "come on down" and be a contestant?**

Choose seven volunteers. Show one student at a time a household or food item and the incorrect price. Ask the contestant to guess whether the item is higher or lower in value than the price tag displayed. Encourage the contestants to involve the audience as much as possible by asking other group members to shout out advice. If the contestant answers correctly, let him or her keep the item. Do this until you have used all seven items.

The second part of the game uses the same principles but involves your entire group. Display two magazine pictures of celebrities. Ask: **If these pictures had a price tag on them, which would be higher and which would be lower in value in the eyes of our culture? Why?** Your students will likely answer that question based on physical attractiveness or recent accomplishments. You might let students vote by applause to determine the more valuable. Do this with several pairs of pictures. Toward the end the game, match the most popular celebrities up

OPTIONS

MOSTLY GIRLS

SHORT MEETING TIME

URBAN

against each other and come up with an MVP (Most Valuable Person). Finally, display some pictures of people the culture considers "unvaluable," match them up against some of the most popular celebrities, and ask students to vote by applause for whom they think is more valuable.

Who is more valuable at your school: popular people or unpopular people? How do you know? What are some ways people in your school show that they value popular people more than unpopular people? (Ask these same types of questions about the athletes, well-dressed students, and other categories of "valued" students at their schools and in their spheres of influence.)

Besides the things we've talked about, at your school what other factors determine whether someone's valuable or not?

How does this method of determining someone's value affect our friendships? (Sometimes there's a price tag put on friendships. If you're not cool enough, you can't be friends with cool people. If you don't have enough value, you can't hang out with people that are valued.)

A lot of people who think like this fall into the Value Trap. They get trapped into thinking that some of their friends have value and some don't. They are nicer to and more interested in people who are popular or smart or "good looking." Do you ever think like this? Do your friendships ever fall into the Value Trap?

Teacher Tip: Sometimes students will deny that the Value Trap exists in their circle of friends, especially those students who want to please you by giving the right "church" answers. One of the best ways to get students to talk about the Value Trap, though, is to ask them to talk about times when *they* felt "unvalued." You might try to prepare one or two students ahead of time to tell stories about how they were treated meanly and unfairly by peers. One honest story may open the floodgates to many more of your students' stories.

STEP 3

Ultimate Affirmation

Below, students act out Jesus' response to the Value Trap in a creative way by using "Value Judges" and funny money.
Or, choose one of the option categories in the sidebar and see pages 39-43 for more "Getting the Word" options.

Supplies needed: cut-out copies of "Funny Money" (Resource 2, page 36), Bibles.
Set up: Prepare a large amount of "Funny Money" by copying Resource 2 on green paper and cutting it into separate bills. Also, prepare students to play the parts of the woman and the four Value Judges in the scene described below.

What would Jesus say about the Value Trap?

Explain that Jesus was confronted by the Value Trap several times during His life. Read Mark 5:21-28 aloud.

Ask the student playing the part of the woman to come to the front of the room with four $10, "Funny Money" bills. One by one, have the Value Judges come in front of her and make a pronouncement. For example, the first judge should pronounce, "She is a woman!" Stop to ask the audience: **Does the fact that she is a woman make her more valuable, less valuable, or neither?** Let students shout out answers. Regardless of what the audience says, have the first Value Judge pronounce, "Unvaluable!" and take a $10 bill away. Do the same thing for the other three judges who should pronounce, respectively: "She is bleeding!"; "She is unable to be healed by doctors"; and "She can't have any contact with other people." Each Value Judge should end by talking $10 away from the girl until she's left with no money. Refer back to the story of the bleeding woman in Mark 5:21-28 and explain that in the culture she lived in, being a woman with incurable bleeding would have made her a social outcast. She would have had virtually no value in her culture.

Read Mark 5:29-34. Help students see the significance of Jesus' action by saying something like: **Jesus looked at a woman who many people labeled "unvaluable," and He affirmed her value in front of everyone there. Jesus proved that she was valuable and gave her something that could never be taken from her.** As dramatically as you can, hand the student playing the part of the woman a stack of $10 bills to represent the value Jesus gave to her.

Imagine you are the woman in the story we just read.

OPTIONS

- LARGE GROUP
- HEARD IT ALL BEFORE
- LITTLE BIBLE BACKGROUND
- FELLOWSHIP & WORSHIP
- MOSTLY GIRLS
- EXTRA FUN
- URBAN

If Jesus affirmed your value right in front of everyone, how would you feel?

Why do you think Jesus treated this woman the way He did? Was there something special about her?

If you wanted to be seen as valuable in Jesus' eyes, what would you have to do? Supplement students' responses by saying something like: **Here is the key: You can't do ANYTHING that will make you any more valued in Jesus' eyes. Jesus already values you more than you can possibly know. Jesus puts no price tags on His friendships!**

But many people don't think of Jesus as a friend. They think that Jesus is just waiting to condemn us for the things we do. Explain that the Bible tells us that Jesus doesn't condemn those that believe in Him. Even though we are all sinners, Jesus never values us any less. Instead, Jesus' great love for us gives us value that no one can ever take away.

In Jesus' eyes, even the unvalued become invaluable. If Jesus has no price tags on His friendships—if He values everyone no matter how smart or good-looking or popular he or she is—how we should treat *our* friends?

2A

Background B - Jewish women value

Jesus Values a Bleeding Woman

Mark 5:21-34

BIBLE BYTES

- BACKGROUND BYTES: According to Jewish law, anyone who touched a woman suffering from menstrual bleeding became "ceremonially unclean" (they would be excluded from worship).
- SCRIPTURE BYTES: For more stories that show how Jesus valued people others labeled "unvaluable," see: Mark 1:40-45; 2:13-17; Luke 7:36-50 and 19:1-9; and John 5:1-15 and 8:1-11.
- BYTE-SIZE INSIGHTS: It's normal for teens to look for value and significance in what they do. This influences everything from the way they dress to the friends they make. But there is only one thing that can satisfy their deep need to know they are loved, valued, and have significance to have relationship with Jesus and experience His love first hand.

STEP 4

How to Be Bleacher Friends

Below, students listen to monologues of unvalued people, then think of ways to encourage those people: 10-15 minutes.
Or, choose one of the option categories in the sidebar and see pages 39-43 for more "Getting the Point" options.

Supplies needed: three copies of Resource 3, "Feeling Unvalued" (page 37), pens, index cards.
Set up: About a week ahead of time, prepare three students to each read one of the monologues from Resource 3. Give them copies of the resource so they can practice.

If you were the woman who was healed by Jesus you would have felt very special. Jesus cheered her on when no one else would. Jesus was a "Bleacher Friend" to the bleeding woman. Have you ever had a Bleacher Friend? Bleacher Friends sit in the bleachers of our life and cheer us on. They encourage us. And they show us and tell us how valuable we are. Has anyone ever been a Bleacher Friend to you? Tell us about it. Let as many students share as you have time for.

You live in a world stuck in the Value Trap. Wouldn't it be a mind-blowing thing if we all decided to break out of the trap and be Bleacher Friends to the people in our lives? What if we decided to be like Jesus and value the unvalued? Have the three students you've prepared read their monologues. While students listen, tell them to think about: **What would Jesus do if He knew these people? How would Jesus show that He values them?**

Pass out pens and index cards and introduce the monologues by saying: Tell students to write an encouraging note on their cards to one of the three unvalued people. When students finish writing, they should get up and give their index cards to the appropriate actor.

Do you think these teens would feel valued by these letters? Why or why not?

Besides writing letters, what else could we do to value these three people?

What kinds of people are unvalued at your school? How can you be Bleacher Friends to them?

Teacher Tip: You may have some students who won't go along with the concept of being "Bleacher Friends." Some students

OPTIONS

LARGE GROUP

LITTLE BIBLE BACKGROUND

SHORT MEETING TIME

JR. HIGH HIGH SCHOOL COMBINED

SIXTH GRADE

may ignore your directions and write harsh and discouraging statements on the cards they give to the actors. (Such can be life in junior high, unfortunately.) This doesn't mean the activity has failed. Since the cards will be anonymous, you have a great opportunity to use the statements as an example of the Value Trap.

other examples of Jesus putting value on the unvalued. Mat 9:9-13 (tax collector) John 8:1-11 (adulteress)

STEP 5

Putting Value into Action

Below, students practice being Bleacher Friends by "cheering on" one another: 5-10 minutes.
Or, choose one of the option categories in the sidebar and see pages 39-43 for more "Getting Personal" options.

Supplies needed: copies of Resource 4, "I Value You," (page 38).
Set up: If possible, have students sit on stairs. The stairs will work as temporary "bleachers" from which students can cheer each other on. If that's not possible, arrange chairs in a semi-circle.

Ask for a volunteer to stand up in front of the rest of the group. Each time a student stands up, lead the rest of the students in loud, rowdy, and encouraging cheers, as if you were cheering on a sports team or a musician at a concert. Discuss what it feels like to be "cheered on." Tell students to remember how much they like to be cheered on and encourage them to remember to cheer on others.

Finally, pass out copies of Resource 4. Encourage students to take it home, fill it out, and send it to someone they want to value. Close in prayer, asking God to help your group become Bleacher Friends.

O P T I O N S

FUNNY MONEY

Photocopy this sheet on green paper and cut these bills apart.

EXTRA ACTION

STEPS 1/2 - TEAM CROSSING

Teams work together to cross the room.

Spread out junk items (newspapers, paper plates, cardboard boxes, etc.) Divide into teams of 7-10. Each team member must make it to the other side of the room by stepping only on the junk. If a student touches the floor, he or she must go back to the start. On each team: blindfold two students, tie up the legs of two, tie up the arms of two, and plug the ears of one. Tell students the key to this activity is valuing each student so that some strong students will have to carry some leg-tied students, etc. Most teams will need about 20 minutes. (Large groups can run two or more courses at the same time.) Ask questions that help teens draw their own conclusions. **Were you tempted at times to feel some teammates were less valuable then others? What did you learn about teamwork? What did you learn about valuing others?** Explain the "Value Trap" concept (see Step 2) and discuss questions like: **What did this game teach us about the Value Trap?** *(Needed: junk items, rope.)*

STEP 5 - ROUND TUIT

An active way to value each other.

Many students *mean* to express value to one another but they never get around to it. Make a "round tuit" for each student by tying the ends of a 3-foot rope together. Scatter several round tuits on the ground and have each student stand in one. Tell half the group to move clockwise and the other group to move counterclockwise and step in as many "round tuits" as time allows. If someone else is in the "round tuit" they step in, they must tell that person an "I value you because. . . ." statement before moving on. Close by telling students how much you value them. *(Needed: ropes.)*

SMALL GROUP

STEPS 1/2 - $5 SHOPPING SPREE

Buy groceries for a family on just $5.

You can help your small group experience what it's like to be unvalued before you talk about valuing others. Arrange to take your group to a grocery store. Assign each group member a family role: parent(s), adolescent(s), grandparent(s), baby. Give your group five dollars (or a five dollar limit) and explain the five dollars must buy food for the whole family for a week. Give students 15-20 minutes to buy the food (or make a list of food items to buy). Discuss what they chose and why, then ask: **If you weren't pretending to be a struggling family and I gave you $5, what *would* you have bought? Was it frustrating to have such a limited budget? How would you feel if you had to live on that budget all the time? Do you ever think about people who actually have to live on $5 per week?** Discuss the "Value Trap." Explain that our culture sees some people—for example people who don't have a lot of money—as less valuable than others. If you had your students buy the food, donate the food to a needy family or shelter. *(Needed: $5, transportation, paper, pencils.)*

STEP 5 - "I VALUE YOU" WEB

Make an "I value you" web by tossing yarn around a circle of students.

This affirmation activity works best in a small group where students know each other well. Bring in a large ball of yarn. Gather teens in a circle. Throw the ball to one student and make an "I value you because. . . ." statement to that student. That student should then hold on to the yarn, throw the ball to a different person, and say something affirming about him or her, and so on. Make sure no one is left out or feels unvalued by the time you're done. *(Needed: yarn.)*

LARGE GROUP

STEP 3 - WIN, LOSE, OR DRAW

Play a variation of the classic game show.

First, divide into groups (girls vs. guys, Central Middle School vs. North Middle School) and play a modified version of "Win, Lose, or Draw." Ahead of time, write the following terms on slips of paper: "skinny," "poor," and "unpopular." Give each team $500 in Funny Money (Resource 2) to start with and put markers and a flip-chart or large piece of newsprint in front of each team. Have one representative come forward from each team. Show the representatives the first clue and have them try to draw it while their team guesses. To demonstrate that each of these clues is something that makes someone less valuable in your students' culture, take $100 *away* from the team that gets the clue right first. Get new students to draw for each clue. Continue with these new clues: "woman" and "bleeding." Explain how these things made the woman in the Bible story less valued in her culture. Then continue with Step 3 as written. *(Needed: pen, slips of paper, flip chart or newsprint, markers.)*

STEP 4 - WWJD STORIES

Small groups brainstorm how Jesus would respond to unvalued students.

In a large group, it might be impractical to read all the ideas from your students' index cards. Huddle up in groups of six to eight. Pass out one copy of Resource 4, blank paper, and pencils to each group. Ask: **What would Jesus do if these unvalued people were His friends?** Then have students write detailed stories of how someone like themselves could be a Bleacher Friend to the unvalued teens. *(Needed: Resource 1, pens, paper.)*

Step 3 - Priceless!

Jesus showed how much He valued us when He died for us.

Students who have heard "Jesus loves and values everyone" all their lives will benefit from this fresh approach. Think about something you (or someone you know) owns that is extremely expensive or valuable (maybe even priceless) that you could bring to your group. Sound risky? It has to be to make the point. For example, one youth worker did this activity with borrowed Super Bowl and airplane tickets. Another showed a diamond that was an irreplaceable family heirloom. One brought currency in an amount students had never seen before. Show and describe the items to the group and explain why they are so valuable to you. During your "show and tell" have an adult come in the room with a small child (preferably one your students know). Have the adult ask about what you're doing. Explain the priceless items, then offer to exchange them for the child. After having a little fun pretending to barter over price ("Come on, the kid is 95% water!"), have the adult turn down the offer and leave. Say: **Obviously, the child is worth more than these priceless items. She's really priceless! That's how Jesus views people: it doesn't matter who or what we have done, He values us for who we are.** *(Needed: valuable items, someone to bring in a baby.)*

Step 5 - Ice Cream on Me

Make coupons to encourage others.

Since students have "heard it all before," challenge them to start living it out. Pass out bright-colored construction paper, scissors and markers and tell students to make "coupons" to give to the friends in their life they want to value. Coupons could be for anything from: "one free ice cream on me" to "one-time room cleaning." *(Needed: markers, construction paper, and scissors.)*

Step 3 - Valued by Jesus

Act out three skits of Jesus valuing the unvalued.

Help students with little Bible background get exposure to more than just one story about how Jesus valued others. Read the following passages: Matthew 9:9-13 (Jesus valued the lowly tax collector, Matthew); Mark 5:25-34 (Jesus valued a bleeding woman); and John 8:1-11 (Jesus valued an adulteress). If you have time, expand the "Value Judges" skit to include Matthew and the adulteress. Or, divide into three groups, assign each group a passage, and ask groups to act out its passage. Discuss: **How do you think these people felt when Jesus valued them? How do you think they responded to Jesus?** Use the end of Step 3 in the main lesson. *(Needed: see Step 3.)*

Step 4 - Response to the Cross

Make a list of ways we can value others and lay it at the foot of a cross.

Set a wooden cross at the front of the room. Discuss: **When we know what great lengths Jesus has gone to value us, how can we respond to Him?** Help students understand how to respond to Christ by detailing how you made Jesus your Leader and Forgiver and how you try to value others because Jesus valued you. Tell students if they want to respond to Christ they can write one of two responses on the backs of their Funny Money (cut-out copies of Resource 2 students should still have from Step 3). First, they might write a letter to Jesus telling Him they want to make Him their Leader and Forgiver. Or, if they have already made that decision, they might write specific ways they can value others, one way on each bill. Have students lay their money at the foot of the cross. *(Needed: cross, Funny Money, pens.)*

Step 3 - Celebrate!

Praise Jesus through writing and singing.

Pass out copies of Resource 4. Tell students to reflect on how much Jesus values them. Have students complete Resource 4 by writing out what they think Jesus might write to them. Choose a few volunteers to share their letters. Then ask students to write letters to Jesus on the back of the resource thanking Jesus for His great love. Ask: **How should we respond to the way Jesus values us?** Lead students in a response time by singing worship songs you're familiar with that celebrate how Jesus values us. Explain that one of the ways students can respond to Jesus is by being Bleacher Friends to other unvalued people. Pass out pens and paper and challenge students to write down the names of one or two people they can be a Bleacher Friend to in the coming week. *(Needed: Bibles, copies of Resource 4, pencils.)*

Step 5 - Friends Forever

Celebrate friends with music and prayer.

For a different ending to the lesson, have students hold hands in a circle and turn the lights in your room down low. Play a meaningful song that celebrates friendship. Next, encourage students to pray out loud as they thank God for their friendships in the group. Make sure no students are left out. *(Needed: candle, CD and CD player or other way to play music.)*

MOSTLY GIRLS

STEP 2 - THE GREAT MAKEOVER

Give one girl a makeover; discuss value.

This activity will capitalize on girls' love for makeovers. Bring in make up and costume accessories. Get permission from one of the students ahead of time and give her a makeover. Call your volunteer to the front of the room and explain to the class that they have 10 minutes to give her a complete makeover. (If you have a large group, you might choose more than one volunteer and divide into makeover teams.) Discuss: **Does she look prettier now? Does she have more value now because she looks prettier? Why or why not? Would most girls at your school think you were more valuable if you were prettier? Do you think Jesus would think you were more valuable if you were prettier? Why or why not? What do you think makes you more valuable to Jesus?** *(Needed: make up and costume accessories.)*

STEP 3 - VALENTINES FROM JESUS

Make valentines from Jesus.

Use the "Value Judges Skit" from the main lesson. Then discuss how much Jesus values each of us today. Say: **We often think we have to look a certain way, wear the best labels, or spend a specific amount of time on ourselves before we have value. That's not true! Jesus values us just the way we are, no matter what we look like, no matter what the rest of the world thinks of us.** If possible, have various Valentine's Day cards to show the students. Explain that we use valentines to show how much we love and value someone. Pass out paper, glue, scissors, and other materials for making valentines. Then have girls make a valentine to themselves as Jesus might have written it. *(Needed: valentines, craft supplies.)*

MOSTLY GUYS

STEP 1 - BLEACHER CHALLENGE

Have guys cheer each other from actual bleachers during a physical challenge.

Guys this age learn best from concrete images and strong object lessons. What if you took your group to a YMCA gym, a local football or soccer field, or some other place where you can all actually sit in some bleachers? Decide on a physical challenge that is difficult but not impossible for your guys. For example, you might have them do 20 push-ups, or you might have them sit back to back, link elbows and require them to stand up without touching the ground. Choose a few volunteers for the challenge. Instruct the rest of the guys NOT to cheer. Then do this a second time with different guys, but this time instruct everyone to encourage and cheer on the volunteers. Refer back to this game when you discuss how important it is to have and be Bleacher Friends who cheer one another on. If possible, continue the rest of the lesson with students sitting on the bleachers. *(Needed: transportation to bleachers.)*

STEP 5 - BLEACHER CHEERS

Cheer each other on from bleachers.

Step 5 can be particularly effective while sitting in a set of actual bleachers. Have guys come down from the bleachers one at a time. When down in front, have each guy share an area of his life where he is facing a challenge or is lacking confidence. Tell the rest of the group to bombard him from the bleachers with encouragement, support, and value. If a particular guy is not ready to share a struggle from his life, that's fine. Just have him stand there and let the group encourage him in whatever way they want. This activity will help your guys feel what it's like to have friends in the bleachers. They won't forget that feeling. *(Needed: transportation to bleachers.)*

EXTRA FUN

STEP 1 - MALLOW MANIA

Play a number of marshmallow games.

Play up the marshmallow theme in Step 1 by using some of the games below. Be sure to end with "Marshmallow Mash," as written in the main lesson to help you transition to Step 2. Try:

- **In Your Face:** Thread string through marshmallows covered with chocolate syrup and dangle them in a doorway or from a pole. Have students race to eat the marshmallows with hands behind backs.
- **Chubby Bunny:** Each round, give contestants one more marshmallow to shove in their mouths (no chewing allowed!), and have them try to say "Chubby Bunny." They're out when they're not audible or when they spit out their mouthful. Hint: have a trash can nearby—VERY nearby!
- **Marshketball:** Yup, it's basketball with marshmallows. Use trash cans for baskets. Play with multiple teams and marshmallows if you have a large group (optimal team size: four or five). No dribbling; you can only take two steps if you have a marshmallow.
- **Marshmallow Sculpture:** Provide lots of marshmallows and toothpicks. Ask teams of three or four to make sculptures.

(Needed: marshmallows, chocolate syrup, trash cans.)

STEP 3 - SCRIPTURE HUNT

Send students out to look for symbols of the main points of the Bible story.

Decide ahead of time what the main points are of the Bible study. Discuss these as a group. Then send kids out in teams to find things that will represent the points. If you have lots of time, take your kids to a grocery store or drug store with $4 per team, and ask them to buy things that will represent the points. If you've got less time (or less $!), send them out in and around your church (or wherever your group meets) with instructions to find things wherever they can. Have the groups share their findings. *(Needed: Bibles, optional: transportation.)*

MEDIA

STEP 1 - TREASURE OF YOU
Reflect on Matthew 13:44-46 and the song "Treasure of You."

The song "Treasure of You" by Stephen Curtis Chapman (on the *Heaven in the Real World* CD) will help students understand how much Jesus values them. Use Step 3, then have someone stand and read Matthew 13: 44-46. When done, ask students to think about whether or not they could actually sell everything they have to follow Christ. As they think about this, play "Treasure of You." If possible, put the lyrics on an overhead and call students' attention to them. When the song is done, confess that you also find it difficult to sell everything to follow Jesus. But then say: **I'm going to read the passage again, but this time I want you to think about the story in a different manner. This time, the treasure is not diamonds or jewels, but it's you that's really the treasure.** Read the passage again. **You see, we are the treasure that Jesus found—and He sold everything He had to buy us. That's how much He values us; He was willing to give it all up for you and me, when He died on the cross.** *(Needed:* Heaven in the Real World *CD and CD player.)*

STEP 5 - CHEERS!
Show a clip from Mr. Holland's Opus.

Mr. Holland's Opus is a powerful movie about the life of a giving orchestra teacher. Cue the scene at the end where Mr. Holland (Richard Dreyfuss) is given a surprise concert by his former students. Show how Mr. Holland basks in the applause of his friends and family. Discuss: **How did Mr. Holland feel at that moment? How did his friends feel? Have you ever helped encourage and thank a friend? How did he or she feel? Who can you think of right now who needs to be cheered for his or her friendship? What can you do to cheer him or her on?** *(Needed: TV, VCR, copy of* Mr. Holland's *Opus.)*

SHORT MEETING TIME

STEP 1 - MAD MONEY SCRAMBLE
Race to gather as many coins as possible.

Instead of playing "Marshmallow Mash," scatter various coins around the room and when all students arrive, have them race to see who can gather the most points (in total value of money gathered). If you don't have a lot of spare change, this can also work with "Funny Money," which you can make by copying Resource 2 on different colored paper. Discuss that assigning different values to different kinds of money is OK, but we sometimes fall into a trap of doing the same thing with people—we think some people have more value than others. *(Needed: coins or "Funny Money.")*

STEP 2 - WHAT'S WORTH MORE?
Students vote on the value of items.

Instead of playing "The Price Is Right," read pairs of items and people and ask students to stand on one wall if they think the first item is more valuable or the other wall if they think the second item is more valuable. For starters: **What's more valuable . . . A family car or a family photo album? A close relative or your best friend? A trophy you earned or an expensive piece of jewelry someone gave you? Brad Pitt or Wesley Snipes? A young teen or a senior citizen?** Use this activity to introduce the Value Trap.

STEP 4 - TEAM BRAINSTORM
Brainstorm ways to value the unvalued.

Skip Resource 3 and brainstorm as a class how you might encourage unvalued people.

STEP 5 - "I VALUE YOU" LETTERS
Send Resource 4 home with students.

Skip the "Bleacher Cheers" activity. Instead, pass out copies of Resource 4 and encourage students to finish it and mail it to a friend. *(Needed: copies of Resource 4.)*

URBAN

STEP 2 - THE RACE IS RIGHT
Compare black and white objects.

In the inner city, racism is a daily reality. This activity will educate teens on the terrible nature of racism which values individuals by skin color. Play "The Race is Right" like "The Price is Right," except each time compare black objects with white objects. Set it up so the white object always has more financial value than the black object. This works best if a few trials are absurd, e.g., a white cupcake vs. a black television. Before long some will realize that the pricing values are in favor of the white items. Before moving on, show some pictures of faces from different ethnicities and let students decide for themselves which face is more valuable. If they already understand that in actuality neither face is more valuable, great! Discuss: **Can color really tell us anything about value?** (No.) **Can one's race or ethnic group tell us anything about a person's value to the world?** (No.) Explain the Value Trap in detail and discuss other ways besides racism people fall into the trap. *(Needed: black items and white items, pictures of faces from a variety of ethnicities.)*

STEP 3 - BLACK MAN AT THE CROSS
Also discuss the story of Simon the Cyrene.

After reading the story of the bleeding woman, read one more story, that of the African, Simon of Cyrene (a country in North Africa), who during Jesus' march to Golgatha helped bear the weight of the cross with Jesus on the Via Dolorosa (see Matthew 27:32, Mark 15:21, and Luke 23:26). To those teens whose cultural self-image is harmed by racism, discussing how Jesus valuing Simon just as much as He did the bleeding woman will help restore an image of ethnic value. *(Needed: see Step 3.)*

COMBINED

STEP 1 - WINNERS & LOSERS

Play any game your students enjoy and show extra value to the winners.

Play any game that will produce a team or individual champion—from football or volleyball to "Bible baseball." Treat the members of the winning team as if they are more valuable than the losers by giving them special privileges and saying especially encouraging things to them. Then discuss: **Is this team really more valuable because it won the game? If not, what really makes someone valuable or not valuable? Do you think people ever get caught up in valuing "winners" more than "losers"? What are some other ways people fall into the "Value Trap" of treating some people like they're more important than others?** *(Needed: variable game supplies.)*

STEP 4 - CUSTOM CASE STUDIES

Teens help create original case studies of unvalued people.

Instead of using the case studies on Resource 4, let your group create its own. Begin by explaining that Driving Dan just got his driver's license, but because he arrived home past his curfew and forgot to fill the car up with gas, his dad and step-mom are about ready to ground him. Ask for a volunteer to share one sentence describing how Driving Dan feels or what he thinks. That volunteer then gets to pick another student who adds a second sentence by building on the thoughts and emotions of the first sentence, and so on until you have 10 sentences. Ask students to think of creative ways they could be a Bleacher Friend and encourage Driving Dan even if he gets grounded. Repeat the process with "New Girl Nancy" by explaining that she has just moved to your neighborhood and although she was popular in her old school, she is having trouble meeting people and often eats lunch alone.

SIXTH GRADE

STEP 1 - M.M. CHEERLEADERS

Add cheerleaders to the teams for the Marshmallow Mash game.

The learning process will be strengthened for your sixth graders if the theme of encouragement is reinforced throughout the session. Ask for two or three volunteers from each team to be a cheering squad for their team during the Marshmallow Mash. Ask them to cheer with words that are encouraging and uplifting. Give cheerleaders their own marshmallows to juggle—and to throw at the other teams. *(Needed: marshmallows.)*

STEP 4 - PRAYER COMMITMENTS

Students commit to pray for at least six friends for a month.

Most sixth graders welcome the challenge of working toward a significant goal. Put several sign-up sheets around the room. Have all students sign one sheet with either something they want the others to pray for or one thing they are thankful for. Pass out paper to each student and have him or her copy from the sign-up sheets the names and prayer requests (or thankful things) of at least six other students. Encourage students to choose names of new friends. Be sure every student is on at least two prayer lists. **When you pray for someone every day for 30 days, you soon realize not only how important that person is to God, but also that he or she is becoming even more important to you. You become interested in how God is answering prayer for that person.** Tell students that you will ask about their prayers each week. Suggest that they post their prayer list somewhere where they will see it each day—on the bathroom mirror, on the refrigerator, on their locker, next to their bed, etc. *(Needed: paper, pencils.)*

PLANNING CHECKLIST

STEP 1 (5-10 MINUTES, UNLESS NOTED)
- ❑ **Extra Action:** Team Crossing* (25-35 min.)
- ❑ **Small Group:** $5 Shopping Spree* (extra time required)
- ❑ **Mostly Guys:** Bleacher Challenge
- ❑ **Extra Fun:** Mallow Mania (15-20 min.)
- ❑ **Media:** Treasure of You
- ❑ **Short Time:** Mad Money Scramble (3-5 min.)
- ❑ **Combined:** Winners and Losers
- ❑ **Sixth Grade:** M.M. Cheerleaders

STEP 2 (10-15 MINUTES, UNLESS NOTED)
- ❑ **Mostly Girls:** The Great Makeover
- ❑ **Short Time:** What's Worth More? (5-10 min.)
- ❑ **Urban:** The Race Is Right

STEP 3 (15-20 MINUTES, UNLESS NOTED)
- ❑ **Large Group:** Win, Lose, or Draw
- ❑ **Heard It All Before:** Priceless!
- ❑ **Little Bible:** Valued by Jesus
- ❑ **Fellowship & Worship:** Celebrate!
- ❑ **Mostly Girls:** Valentines from Jesus
- ❑ **Extra Fun:** Scripture Hunt
- ❑ **Urban:** Black Man at the Cross

STEP 4 (10-15 MINUTES, UNLESS NOTED)
- ❑ **Large Group:** WWJD Stories
- ❑ **Little Bible:** Response to the Cross
- ❑ **Short Time:** Team Brainstorm (5 min.)
- ❑ **Combined:** Custom Case Studies
- ❑ **Sixth Grade:** Prayer Commitments

STEP 5 (5-10 MINUTES, UNLESS NOTED)
- ❑ **Extra Action:** Round Tuit
- ❑ **Small Group:** "I Value You" Web
- ❑ **Heard It All Before:** Ice Cream on Me
- ❑ **Fellowship & Worship:** Friends Forever
- ❑ **Mostly Guys:** Bleacher Cheers
- ❑ **Media:** Cheers!
- ❑ **Short Time:** "I Value You" Letters (5 min.)

** two combined steps*

SESSION

3 Second-Chance Friends

YOUR GOALS FOR THIS SESSION:

Choose one or more

- [ ] To help students learn that Jesus forgave Peter's big mistake.
- [ ] To help students understand a mind-blowing idea about forgiveness: Jesus gives all of us more chances than we deserve.
- [ ] To challenge students to become Second-Chance Friends—friends that forgive people like Jesus did.
- [ ] Other ______________________________

____

Your Bible Base:

Mark 14:27-31
Mark 14:43-50
Mark 14:66-72
~~Mark 15:16-72~~
~~Luke 23:32-43~~
John 21:1-19

STEP 1

Unhand Me!

OPTIONS

Below, students try to master two challenges while "handcuffed": 5-10 minutes. Or, choose one of the option categories in the sidebar and see pages 55-59 for more "Getting Together" options.

Supplies needed: rope—one 2-foot piece for each student (or towels, rubber bands, or hair ties), gum.
Set up: Divide into two teams by age, gender, or at random, and "handcuff" the teams together. To do this, give each student a piece of rope. Students should tie one end of the rope to one of their own wrists and the other end of the rope to the closest wrist of the person next to them. You will probably have to walk around the room and help tie the students' wrists together. The end result is that each team becomes a line of people whose adjoining hands are tied together.

Give each student a piece of gum. Each team member must unwrap, chew, and blow a bubble with the gum. The first team done wins. This is much harder than it seems because it requires students to work together.

The first team to do 20 relatively normal-looking jumping jacks, wins. This one is certain to produce hilarious results.

NOTE: Don't let students untie the ropes just yet. It's important to let them experience the feeling of being "handcuffed" throughout the lesson.

Teacher Tip: If you can't find enough rope, give each student a towel. Students should grab one end of one towel with their left hands, then with their right hands grab the open end of the towel held by the person on their right. If any student lets go during one of the challenges above, his or her team must start over.

STEP 2

The Friendship Graveyard

Below, students write names of "dead" friendships on tombstones: 10-15 minutes. Or, choose one of the option categories in the sidebar and see pages 55-59 for more "Getting Thirsty" options.

Supplies needed: copies of Resource 5, "Friendship Tombstone" (page 51), pens or pencils, tape.

Have students discuss the following questions with one or two people next to them: **Just now, you experienced a little bit of what it's like to feel "handcuffed." And while we may not know what it's like to truly be handcuffed, there are things that handcuff our friendships, too—things that bind our friendships and keep them from growing. Not forgiving is like that. We like to hold grudges and stay angry at our friends, but we never realize that not only does this handcuff us, it slowly (or not so slowly) kills our friendship.**

Think for a moment about the friendships that have died in your life. I'm not talking about friendships where one person physically moves away or moves on to another school, job, or stage of life. I'm talking about situations when a good friendship goes bad because one mistake or source of conflict was never dealt with. Ask students to think of a friendship that was handcuffed and eventually died.

Pass out pens and copies of Resource 5. Instruct students to complete the resource with a short summary of why one friendship from their past ended up in the Friendship Graveyard. This will be difficult for students to do while they're tied up, but not impossible if they work together. After three or four minutes, collect the friendship tombstones and tape them to one of your walls.

We've created quite a Friendship Graveyard here. What might have saved these friendships, or brought them back to life? What would have given them a second chance? It's pretty simple actually. No matter how much a friend has hurt us, or no matter how much we have hurt a friend, there *is* something that can bring a friendship back to life. It's forgiveness. Imagine how different this wall would look if forgiveness could bring these friendships back to life.

OPTIONS

- LITTLE BIBLE BACKGROUND
- EXTRA FUN
- MEDIA
- URBAN
- JR. HIGH / HIGH SCHOOL COMBINED

STEP 3

The Great Debate

OPTIONS

Below, students debate whether or not Jesus should forgive Peter. 15-20 minutes. Or, choose one of the option categories in the sidebar and see pages 55-59 for more "Getting the Word" options.

Supplies needed: paper, pens, white board or newsprint, marker, copies of Resource 5, "Friendship Tombstone" (page 51), scissors or a knife.

Explain: **Jesus is our model for what makes a good friendship. If we want to know how to survive the Friendship Graveyard, we need look no further than how Jesus dealt with forgiveness**. Read the following Scripture passages aloud and ask students to come up with a one-sentence summary statement of each passage. Sample summary statements are included in parentheses below. Record answers on white board or newsprint.

- Mark 14:27-31 (Jesus predicted Peter's denial).
- Mark 14:43-50 (Jesus was arrested and all the disciples—including Peter—abandoned Jesus).
- Mark 14:66-72 (Peter denied Jesus three times, then wept about it).
- Mark 15:16-32 (Jesus was mocked and crucified).

Tell students to imagine the scene after Jesus' resurrection when Jesus met with Peter again. Ask: **If you were Jesus, would you still be angry with Peter for deserting you while you hung on the cross?** Set up a debate to decide whether or not Jesus should forgive Peter. Students should still be in two teams tied together at the wrists. Make one team the "YES" team (defending the position that Jesus SHOULD forgive Peter) and the other the "NO" team (arguing that Jesus SHOULD NOT forgive Peter). Explain that each team should make a list of all the arguments that support its side. Explain that even if students don't necessarily agree with the position that they've been assigned, as good debaters their job is to come up with the best possible arguments anyway. If possible, ask adults to help the students to determine and refine their best arguments. Then let the teams express their opinions in a standard debate format: one representative from the YES team tells why Jesus should forgive, then a representative from the NO team gives a rebuttal, and so on. Read what Jesus did in John 21:1-19.

What did Jesus mean when He said, "Feed my sheep"? (Jesus had trained Peter to be a leader of the forthcoming Church. Jesus was telling Peter to go and do what he had been trained for—to shepherd Jesus' "sheep"—the people who would decide to follow Jesus. Essentially, Jesus was saying, "I'm not going to hold a grudge against you. I forgive you and I'll give you a second chance.")

Do you think forgiveness was hard or easy for Jesus? Why?

What can we learn about overcoming the Friendship Graveyard from the way Jesus forgave Peter?

Jesus put up with people mocking Him, spitting on Him, calling Him names. He endured hanging on the cross, the most brutal way to die in the society in which He lived. And in the meantime, He had to suffer while His best friends on earth deserted Him. Jesus had every right to be flaming mad. Instead, Jesus did something incredible. He forgave Peter. He let Peter know that they would still be friends and partners in ministry. Did you know that same forgiveness extends to you and to me? Isn't that a mind-blowing idea? Untie or cut loose half of students' wrists so that students end up tied to one partner, instead of to a whole team. **If Jesus forgave us like that, how could we NOT forgive others?**

Optional: Help students *experience* the idea that the forgiveness Jesus gave Peter extends to them as well. Pass out additional copies of Resource 5, "Friendship Tombstone." Have students write down just one wrong thing they've done at some point in their past. (Again, this will be difficult but not impossible while they are tied at the wrists.) Explain that even if students had lived a perfect life except for the one thing on their tombstones, that one thing would still be enough to send their friendship with Jesus to the "graveyard." Tell students to close their eyes and imagine how full their tombstones would be if they wrote down *everything* they ever did wrong. Tell students that the sins they are thinking about are the reason Jesus died on the cross. While students keep their eyes closed, try to describe some of the things Jesus might have been thinking about as He hung on the cross. Make it as personal as you can for the students—Jesus may have thought about them and their sins. As you speak, walk around and tear up each of the "Tombstone" resources.

BIBLE BYTES

Jesus Forgives Peter

John 21:1-19

- BACKGROUND BYTES: When Jesus met with Peter and the other disciples for the first time after His resurrection, He performed the same miracle He did when He first called Peter, Andrew, James, and John to be His full-time disciples. (He provided them with an enormous catch of fish; see Luke 5:1-11.) • Jesus asked Peter, "Do you love me?" three times because three times Peter had denied Jesus.
- SCRIPTURE BYTES: For more direct teaching on forgiveness, see: 1 John 1:9, Acts 10:43, and Ephesians 1:7. For passages that encourage students to forgive others as they have been forgiven, see: Ephesians 4:32, Luke 6:37, Colossians 3:13, and Matthew 18:23-35.
- BYTE-SIZE INSIGHTS: God's work in a person's life creates a forgiving heart. As students grow closer to God they will become more willing to give up their own "rights" in order to keep a friendship from ending up in the Friendship Graveyard.

STEP 4

How to Be a Second-Chance Friend

Below, students list the consequences of not forgiving others. Also, students' wrists are finally cut loose: 10-15 minutes.
Or, choose one of the option categories in the sidebar and see pages 55-59 for more "Getting the Point" options.

OPTIONS

- SMALL GROUP
- LARGE GROUP
- LITTLE BIBLE BACKGROUND
- FELLOWSHIP & WORSHIP
- MOSTLY GIRLS
- MOSTLY GUYS

Supplies needed: pens, slips of paper, white board (or newsprint), marker, scissors or a knife to cut the rope off of students' wrists.
Set up: Write out about six situations that your students would find hard to forgive, each on its own slip of paper. For example:

- My friend told a lie about me to impress some popular kids.
- My friend borrowed $10 from me and never paid it back.
- My friend ruined my favorite CD that I loaned him (or her).
- My little brother is a pest and a pain.

Give each slip of paper to one student.

The students who have the slips of paper should take turns reading the situations listed on those sheets. For each situation, two or three other people should call back with negative consequences for not forgiving a friend in that situation. For example, students might call back: You'll stay angry; you won't want to see your friend at school; you won't want to sit next to her in class. Make a list of all the negative consequences students come up with for not forgiving. Put this on a white board or newsprint.

Direct students' attention to the list and say: **This is quite a list. Wouldn't it be good to be free of all of this?** Hold up one students' free hand and say: **We've been cut free from *our* mistakes by what Jesus did for us. Why would we want to stay handcuffed with our other hand because we don't want to forgive others? When we don't forgive other people, our handcuffs are our bitterness and anger toward the people who have wronged us. Saying "I forgive you" cuts us free from these consequences.** Go around the room and untie or cut loose the ropes that tie pairs of students together.

What you've just experienced is how it feels to be a Second-Chance friend. Second-Chance friends are friends that forgive others whether or not it seems "fair" at the time. They give up their grudges, like Jesus did. It's often hard to forgive our friends. Are you willing to be a friend like Jesus?

STEP 5

Putting Forgiveness into Action

Below, students write letters of forgiveness: 10-15 minutes.
Or, choose one of the option categories in the sidebar and see pages 55-59 for more "Getting Personal" options.

Supplies needed: copies of Resource 6, "I Forgive You" (page 53), pens.

Pass out pens and copies of Resource 6. Challenge students to write a letter expressing forgiveness of someone they have bitterness toward. Introduce the letter-writing activity by saying something like: **Many of us have been carrying around the weight of unforgiveness for years. Maybe a friend hurt our feelings or a teacher blamed us for something we didn't do. What seems fair at first is not to forgive that person. But if you choose not to forgive, you end up in handcuffs. Today is your chance to be a Second-Chance Friend and move on in freedom. If you're ready, write a letter on the resource sheet to a person you need to forgive. It's up to you whether or not you ever give this letter to the person. What is most important is that you sincerely forgive the other person in your own heart.**

After students finish writing their letters, refer back to the Friendship Graveyard on your wall (from Step 2). Give students a chance to pull the tombstones off the wall if they are ready to forgive the person that took the friendship to the graveyard in the first place. Give students the option of doing this silently. But some students will be ready to talk about their commitments. Encourage them to explain what friendship they're committing to forgive and what step they will take toward restoring the friendship.

Close in prayer, thanking Jesus for the way He forgives us which allows us to forgive our friends.

OPTIONS

FRIENDSHIP TOMBSTONE

REST IN PEACE

This friendship died because:

I Forgive You

I don't want to handcuff our friendship anymore.
I FORGIVE YOU. Here's what I need to say to you:

EXTRA ACTION

STEPS 1/2 - EGG DROP

Give students an impossible challenge.

Divide into teams of four to six students in each. Give each team an egg, a piece of newspaper, two straws, and three inches of masking tape. Tell teams to create a protective structure around the egg so that the egg can survive a fall from the top of an eight-foot ladder without cracking. This is an impossible challenge. Use provoking questions to engage students' feelings when they fail: **Did anyone feel angry toward a teammate? Why? What does it feel like to fail? What does it feel like when other people fail us? What should you do when you experience failure?** Give teams a second chance—this time with more materials: one egg, a whole newspaper, six straws, and 12 inches of masking tape. Students should be able to create enough protection around the egg so it can survive the fall. Continue to discuss: **How did you feel when you were given a second chance? Do we need second chances in life? When? If we all need second chances, why is it so hard for us to give people who hurt us second chances?** *(Needed: eggs, newspapers, straws, masking tape, ladder.)*

STEP 5 - DROP ZONE

Students drop letters into the "drop zone."

Pass out copies of Resource 6 and have students write letters to someone they need to forgive. Have students drop the letters from the top of a ladder to a "drop zone." To make the drop zone: Use rope or tape to mark off four concentric circles on a small tarp or blanket. Ask for volunteers to share about what they wrote. *(Needed: copies of Resource 6, pencils, ladder, tarp or blanket, tape or rope.)*

SMALL GROUP

STEPS 1/2 - PRISON VISION

Take a trip to a local prison.

In a small group, it's easier to arrange to meet in an off-site location. Take advantage of this and begin with a tour of a local jail or correctional facility. Many facilities will be happy to comply. Be sure to inform parents of your plans. Finish your meeting in a conference room or lobby. Discuss: **Can criminals be forgiven? Can a mass murderer like Charles Manson or the Unabomber be forgiven? Do some people deserve forgiveness but others don't? How do you know when someone deserves forgiveness? Have any of you ever experienced undeserved forgiveness? How did it feel? Can God forgive criminals? Why would He?** *(Needed: transportation or special arrangements.)*

STEP 3 - DID HE DESERVE IT?

Discuss if Peter deserved forgiveness.

If the debate would not work for your small group, read the Scripture together and discuss whether or not Peter "deserved" Jesus' forgiveness. Help students see that none of us really deserves Jesus' forgiveness—He's Holy and we are sinners. Use the optional activity at the end of Step 3 to reinforce this idea. *(Needed: see Step 3.)*

STEP 4 - CUFFED!

Discuss forgiving others in depth.

In a small group, you have an opportunity for deeper discussion. Try to bring in a pair of real handcuffs. (Toy cuffs will also work.) Sit in a circle, hold the cuffs, and (without mentioning names) talk about a person in your life who has been hard to forgive; tell how not forgiving the person has made you feel "handcuffed." Then pass the cuffs around the circle and encourage each person to share a similar story (but don't force anyone). Ask follow-up questions like: **What makes it hard to forgive? After today are you willing to forgive?** *(Needed: handcuffs.)*

LARGE GROUP

STEP 1 - TEAM CHALLENGES

Volunteers compete in the handcuffed challenges for their teams.

In a large group, it might be difficult to handcuff all your students. Instead, you can create energy and momentum by dividing into teams according to schools or gender. Choose three members per team for each of the bubble gum and jumping jack challenges and tie the wrists of the contestants for each team together. Encourage the "audience" to cheer for the respective team representatives. Consider giving a prize (like a bag of candy to share) to the winning team. *(Needed: rope, team prize.)*

STEP 4 - FORGIVEN INTERVIEWS

Interview students who have experienced God creating a forgiving heart.

To stimulate discussion, prepare two or three students to give testimonies about how God has created in them a more forgiving heart. For best results, interview the students. This gives you a little more control in helping guide students to hit the important points of their stories. It's also a less intimidating format for students who may not be comfortable speaking to a large group. Use questions like: **What was it like before you had a forgiving heart? Did you ever feel "handcuffed" because you weren't willing to forgive others? When did you come to understand Jesus' unconditional forgiveness for you? Did it become easier to forgive others then? Why? What's one example of someone you forgave recently? What did that feel like?** After the interviews, break down into small groups and use the first activity in Step 4. *(Needed: see Step 4.)*

OPTIONS

S E S S I O N T H R E E

Step 1 - Off the Cuff
Stage a phony arrest—of yourself!

To start the meeting, explain that you're a little frustrated because of a slight traffic "incident" on your way in. Arrange for a police officer to enter your room, act as if he or she recognizes you, then handcuff you and read your rights. Explain that it was all just a gag. But prepare the officer to refuse to release you. Instead, continue to talk to the students and explain to them how difficult it is to express yourself with your hands cuffed. Refer back to this when you talk throughout the lesson about how holding grudges "handcuffs" our friendships. You might be amazed how many police officers enjoy playing along to make a point. It might help to persuade an officer on the idea if you invite him or her to give a five-minute talk on law enforcement, who gets handcuffed, whether it's fun to arrest youth workers, etc. Oh, and be sure to tell the senior pastor about your plans. *(Needed: handcuffs, guest police officer.)*

Step 3 - Forgive Who?
Debate: Should Jesus forgive a murderer?

Your group may take Jesus' forgiveness for granted. Instead of debating whether Jesus should forgive Peter, research the story of a real-life, hardened criminal, and send a summary of the story to your students in the week ahead of time. Include the question: **Should Jesus forgive him?** (This has the added benefit of promoting your meeting.) Use the same debate format described in the lesson. After the debate, read Luke 2:39-43 and 1 John 1:9. Make the point that the hardened criminal doesn't deserve Jesus' forgiveness, but Jesus certainly *would* forgive him. Then explain that God doesn't rank sins and all of us are just as sinful as the murderer you debated—we all fall short of God's glory (Romans 3:9-18). Use the optional activity to reinforce this. *(Needed: letters to send to students; for additional supplies, see Step 3.)*

Step 2 - Will Jesus Forgive Me?
Watch one student perform a monologue.

It may be important for your group to first focus on the question, "Will Jesus forgive me?" Prepare one student to perform a dramatic monologue. The character should explain feeling handcuffed by sin. In a conversation with God, the actor should wonder out loud whether Jesus could ever forgive his or her sins. Pass out copies of Resource 5, but have students fill out the resource by writing about the sins that keep them "handcuffed" with God. *(Needed: copies of Resource 5.)*

Step 3 - Mock Trial
Hold a mock trial for an average teen.

Hold a trial to determine if Jesus should forgive an average young teen for his or her sins. Have the students determine a "crime" common to junior highers: cheating, lying, etc. Then break the students into the "defense" team (which argues the defendant should be forgiven) and the "prosecution" team (which argues the defendant should not be forgiven). A student playing the part of defendant should admit to the crime and be repentant. When both sides have finished, you (playing the part of judge) should read 1John 1:9 and declare the defendant "forgiven." Then use the optional activity in Step 3. *(Needed: see Step 3.)*

Step 4 - As East Is from West
Burn sins written on paper.

Give students an opportunity to confess their sins to God. Have students write their sins on slips of paper and pray silently, asking Jesus to forgive them. Have students place their folded papers in a metal container and have a leader ignite the paper and let it burn until it's gone (this is best done outside with proper safety precautions). Read Jeremiah 31:34b and Psalm 103:12. Lead into Step 5 by saying: **If Jesus forgives us, shouldn't we forgive others?** *(Needed: paper, pens, container, matches.)*

Step 1 - Depth Groups
Discuss friendship in small groups.

If your group would rather start with discussion than a game, divide into "depth groups" (optimal size: four to six students each). Ask groups to come up with a list of qualities that make a great friendship and another list of things that can ruin a friendship. Then have group members discuss: **How have you felt when a friendship has ended? Was there anything you could have done to save the friendship? Was there anything the other person could have done?** This will transition to Step 2, where you will discuss that forgiveness can save friendships from the "graveyard."

Step 4 - Communion
Share the Lord's Supper together.

After talking about the way Jesus forgives us, what better way to worship than to hold a student communion service? Talk to leaders in your church to 1) see if this is appropriate and 2) get instruction on how your church administers the Lord's Supper. Since forgiving others is an important part of preparing for the Lord's Supper, pass out copies of Resource 6 and give students a few minutes to write a letter to anyone they need to forgive. This is a great chance for you to teach how God's forgiveness of our sins is intricately connected with our forgiveness of others (see Matthew 6:14 and 18:21-25). Then lead your students in communion. *(Needed: copies of Resource 6, communion elements.)*

Step 5 - The Forgiveness Verse
Meditate on Ephesians 4:32.

Have students write forgiveness letters as directed in the main lesson. Then, turn the lights down. Ask students to look up Ephesians 4:32 in their Bibles and spend time meditating on and memorizing the verse. Encourage them to ask God to provide courage to forgive the friends who have hurt them. *(Needed: See Step 5.)*

MOSTLY GIRLS

Step 3 - Peter's Journal

Record Peter's thoughts on paper.

Instead of using the Great Debate idea, read the Scripture listed in Step 3 and have girls record what Peter might have been thinking after each scene. You'll especially want to focus on how he might have felt after he denied Jesus three times and how he felt after Jesus forgave him. At the end of the Scripture reading, let a few volunteers share their journal entries. *(Needed: pens, paper.)*

Step 4 - Second Chance?

Decide whether the girls in case studies deserve a second chance.

The most effective way to teach girls about forgiveness is to show them real-life examples. Write the following situations each on their own index cards:

- You are a basketball player. Jill, the star of your team, needed to pass her History test so she could play in the game today. She got caught using a cheat sheet, failed the test, and was disqualified from the game. Your team lost the big game by four points. Does Jill deserve a second chance?
- You've been trying to be nice to the new girl, Kelly. In fact, you invited her to a sleepover. She was supposed to bring over two movies, but she forgot about the sleepover and didn't come at all. All your friends were mad at *you* because they couldn't watch the movies. Does Kelly deserve a second chance?
- Come up with additional situations as you like.

Pass out the cards. Whoever gets a card should read it. Then discuss: **Would it be hard or easy to forgive the person? How might you feel "handcuffed" if you didn't forgive? What are some of the consequences you would have to deal with if you didn't forgive?** *(Needed: index cards, pens.)*

MOSTLY GUYS

Step 1 - Two-Man Challenges

Compete while "handcuffed" to a partner.

Have students compete in the "Handcuffed Challenges" in Step 1 while tied at the wrist to just one partner. Time the guys, award one point for the fastest duo in each challenge, and keep track of an overall winner. In addition to the challenges in Step 1, add these: tie/untie your shoes, do 10 sit-ups, write or draw something, make a pyramid of paper cups, hit a baseball off a tee, shoot a basketball into a hoop. *(Needed: gum, pencils, paper cups, baseball, tee, basketball, hoop or trash can.)*

Steps 4/5 - Hands-on Reminders

Make one of two physical reminders.

While students do one of the two "hands on" activities below, read Matthew 18:21-25 and discuss questions like: **Why is it hard to forgive someone if he or she wrongs you more than once? Why is it hard to forgive someone if it doesn't seem like he or she is sorry?**

- Serve Crosses: Have guys bring in pocket knives from home and "whittle" sticks while you discuss forgiveness. (Review safety rules—the most important are to always cut down and away, and to treat the knife with respect, not as a toy. Insist on strict compliance.) Carve or write the word "deserve" into the sticks, then discuss the fact that Jesus forgave us though we didn't deserve it. Crack or cut the sticks in half between the letters "e" and "s" so that the word "serve" is now on one section of the sticks. Tie the two sections of stick with twine to make a cross. *(Needed: Pocket knives, sticks, twine.)*
- Give each student a block of wood. Tell him to write on it the initials of people who are hard to forgive. Toward the end of the discussion, bring out some wood burners and have each guy burn a large "70 x 7" on the word over the initials he wrote there, reminding him that Jesus said to forgive others not seven times but 70 times 7. *(Needed: wood, pens, wood burners.)*

EXTRA FUN

Step 1 - Obstacle Course

Lead teams through an obstacle course while team members are tied up.

Use the bubble gum and jumping jacks challenges to begin, then lead your teams to an obstacle course you've set up. (If you have a large group, you may want to divide into more teams.) Ideally, you'll want to set up your obstacle course outside. If you have a children's playground at your church or you can access one at a nearby park or school, it will make a great obstacle course. Otherwise, you could set up one in your meeting room using a creative arrangement of chairs and tables. Walk through the course yourself first, or have an untied student walk it as you direct. Make sure the obstacle course is difficult enough, but remember that the students will have limited use of their hands. "Spot" the teams as they move through the most precarious elements to ensure that no one gets hurt. *(Needed: some kind of obstacle course. For additional supplies, see Step 1.)*

Step 2 - Tombstone Rubbings

Visit a cemetery and "rub" tombstones.

Take your group to a cemetery and have the students make tombstone rubbings to set up the "Friendship Graveyard" exercise described in the lesson. Give each student a few pieces of paper (larger paper works better) and a crayon. Have each student fold the paper on the front of a tombstone, then rub the side of the crayon across it. The raised or recessed writing on the tombstone will show up in color on the paper. After this exercise, take advantage of the setting and switch gears from Extra Fun to Extra Serious. Have students walk around the graveyard silently and think about friendships that have "died" because of a lack of forgiveness. Throw out questions for them to think about silently like: **What could you have done to save the friendship?** *(Needed: crayons, large sheets of paper, transportation.)*

STEP 2 - MEDIA INTRODUCTION

Use one of three media options.

After playing a lighthearted game like "Handcuffed Challenges," use one of these ideas to transition to the heart of the lesson:

- **Forgiveness Interviews:** Make a home video of teens talking about either a time they were forgiven or a time they forgave someone. If possible, edit the video so that the clips start with people talking about situations that are hard to forgive, then moves to people talking about how freeing it is or was for them to forgive a friend.
- **Contemporary Song:** Play a song that has a forgiveness theme, like "Will You Forgive?" by the Newsboys on the *Take Me to Your Leader* CD.
- **Movie clip:** Play a scene or two from a move popular with your students and appropriate for your meeting that shows either: 1) A dramatic portrayal of forgiveness, or 2) A scene in which two friends have a hard time forgiving one another.

Whichever option you choose, discuss questions like: **Is it easy or hard to forgive? Why? What happens when we don't forgive others?** *(Needed: TV, VCR, home video or movie; or CD player, CD.)*

STEP 1 - UNTANGLE

Grab arms, then try to get untangled.

Instead of taking the time to tie students' hands together, begin by having students stand in a circle. Tell students to reach across the circle and grab the wrists of two other people. Then see how long it takes for students to get untangled—they cannot let go of the wrists they are holding; the goal is to end up back in a circle where each person stands next to the two people he or she is holding wrists with. Discuss: **What are some things that "tangle" our friendships? What can untangle our friendships?**

STEP 3 - PROS AND CONS

Brainstorm reasons why Jesus should or should not forgive a criminal.

As a group, read Luke 23:32-42 aloud—instead of the story of Jesus and Peter, this is the story of how Jesus forgave a criminal hanging on a cross next to Him. Keep students together in one group. Ask your students to brainstorm a few reasons why Jesus should NOT forgive the criminal. Then ask them to brainstorm a few reasons why Jesus SHOULD forgive the criminal. Read Luke 23:43 and then discuss: **Why did Jesus forgive the criminal? Do you think He should have? Why or why not?** Stress the fact that Jesus forgave the criminal, even though the criminal didn't deserve it.

STEP 5 - SEND IT HOME!

Send Resource 6 home with students.

If you're out of time at the end of the session, send students home with Resource 6 and have them fill it out on their own.

STEP 2 - REAL GRAVEYARDS

Discuss the reality that many urban teens' friends may have literally died.

Many urban teens have witnessed or know of someone who has been murdered or otherwise died tragically. In preparation for the "Friendship Graveyard" discussion, ask the group: **How many of you know of someone who has been killed or murdered, especially someone close to you?** Secondly, ask if anyone has lost a friend or loved one to disease or illness. Afterward, discuss the power friendships have on us and how we must value friends and family members while they are here with us. Finally, use Resource 5 and the concluding comments at the end of Step 2. *(Needed: see Step 2.)*

STEP 3 - FORGIVING JUDAS

Study Judas's betrayal.

Forgiving Peter is one thing, but what about the Judas in your life? Many city teens are living with Post Traumatic Stress Syndrome (PTSS). That is, they've witnessed murder or have been the victims of sexual or drug violence, police brutality, neglect, and abuse to name a few atrocities. Many teens can forgive the Peters in their lives—i.e., friendships which tear because of cowardice in commitments. But, true freedom can't emerge until they can forgive the Judases who have betrayed them outright, such as a parent who walked out of their lives or the murderer who killed a family member. This level of forgiveness is needed because much of their present stress, anger, and trauma may be related to not forgiving those who have wounded them forever. Give a short Bible study comparing Judas' betrayal (Matthew 26—27; Mark 14; John 18); Jesus' statement of forgiveness on the cross (Luke 23:34); and His mandate to forgive enemies (Matthew 5:44, Luke 6:27). *(Needed: Bibles.)*

COMBINED

SIXTH GRADE

PLANNING CHECKLIST

STEP 1 - ON THE ROCKS

Use rocks to symbolize the consequences of not forgiving others.

As an alternative to the "handcuffs" theme, give each student two rocks. For best results, give out the rocks one week ahead of time, and require students to carry the rocks around with them no matter where they go on the day before your meeting. The more frustrated they are with the rocks by the time of the meeting, the better. Use the rocks as a symbol of the consequences of unforgiveness wherever the lesson talks about "handcuffs." Instead of playing "Handcuffed Challenges" in Step 1, try the same challenges while students hold the rocks. Later, talk about how Jesus took one of our rocks away—He forgave us of our sins. Now we need to get rid of our other rock by forgiving others. *(Needed: rocks.)*

STEP 2 - MOCK ARGUMENT

Simulate an argument.

Instead of filling out the "Friendship Tombstones," this idea will get students talking about their friendship conflicts: Simulate an argument with a student or adult. For example, you might argue with another adult leader about how the "Handcuffed Challenges" in Step 1 should have been done. In the mock argument that ensues, make reference to the fact that there's a larger issue under the surface—something for which the two of you haven't forgiven each other. Don't let anyone else know what's going on. Start to go on with the meeting as if nothing happened, then stop a few minutes later as if you're just too distraught about it to go on. Ask students for advice. See if anyone advises you to forgive the person. Then admit that it was all an act. This simulation should make students more ready to talk about their own experiences with hard-to-forgive situations.

STEP 1 - WILTING WORDS

Make a chain of hurtful words and see whether it's possible to escape.

Have a large number of plastic grocery bags and permanent markers available. Ask the students to write on the grocery bags some words or phrases of things that can damage friendships. Begin a chain by tying the ends of one bag together to make a loop. Then connect another bag by tying it through the loop of the first bag and continue this process to form a chain of words. Have the students tie all their chains together to form one long chain. Seat two volunteers on chairs back to back and carefully put the chain of words all the way around both of them and the chairs. Talk about the words that have been written on the bags. **What effect could any of these words have on a friendship? Do you think these words really hurt? Is this permanent or would you be able to get out the chain? How can you get out of words or actions that hurt a friendship?** (Forgiveness.) *(Needed: plastic grocery bags, markers, chairs.)*

STEP 5 - FORGIVE ACROSTIC

Make an acrostic with forgiving words.

Distribute paper and pencils, and instruct the students to write the letters to the words "I FORGIVE" down the left side of the paper. Explain that they are to write a word or phrase about forgiveness by using each letter in those words. For example, on the line with the letter F, write "God **F**orgives me." Ask for volunteers to read what they have written.Talk about how we learn about forgiveness from Jesus' example. *(Needed: pens, paper.)*

STEP 1 (5-10 MIN. UNLESS NOTED)

- ❑ **Extra Action:** Egg Drop* (25 min.)
- ❑ **Small Group:** Prison Vision* (extra time needed)
- ❑ **Large Group:** Team Challenges
- ❑ **Heard It All Before:** Off the Cuff
- ❑ **Fellowship & Worship:** Depth Groups
- ❑ **Mostly Guys:** Two-Man Challenges
- ❑ **Extra Fun:** Obstacle Course (15-20 min.)
- ❑ **Short Time:** Untangle (5 min.)
- ❑ **Combined:** On the Rocks
- ❑ **Sixth:** Wilting Words

STEP 2 (10-15 MIN. UNLESS NOTED)

- ❑ **Little Bible:** Will Jesus Forgive Me?
- ❑ **Extra Fun:** Tombstone Rubbings (extra time needed)
- ❑ **Media:** Media Introduction
- ❑ **Urban:** Real Graveyards
- ❑ **Combined:** Mock Argument

STEP 3 (15-20 MIN. UNLESS NOTED)

- ❑ **Small Group:** Did He Deserve It?
- ❑ **Heard It All Before:** Forgive *Who?*
- ❑ **Little Bible:** Mock Trial
- ❑ **Mostly Girls:** Peter's Journal
- ❑ **Short Time:** Pros and Cons (10 min.)
- ❑ **Urban:** Forgiving Judas

STEP 4 (10-15 MIN. UNLESS NOTED)

- ❑ **Small Group:** Cuffed!
- ❑ **Large Group:** Forgiven Interviews
- ❑ **Little Bible:** As East Is from West
- ❑ **Fellowship & Worship:** Communion
- ❑ **Mostly Girls:** Second Chance?
- ❑ **Mostly Guys:** Hands-On Reminders*

STEP 5 (5-10 MIN. UNLESS NOTED)

- ❑ **Extra Action:** Drop Zone
- ❑ **Fellowship & Worship:** The Forgiveness Verse
- ❑ **Short Time:** Send It Home!
- ❑ **Sixth:** Forgive Acrostic

SESSION 4

Fox-Hole Friends

YOUR GOALS FOR THIS SESSION:

Choose one or more

- [ ] To help students learn that Jesus held the disciples accountable during an intense time in the Garden of Gethsemane.
- [ ] To help students understand a mind-blowing idea about accountability: Jesus wanted the support of the friends who lived in the "fox hole" with Him.
- [ ] To help students become Fox-Hole Friends—friends that keep each other accountable to specific spiritual goals.
- [ ] Other: ______________________________

Your Bible Base

Matthew 26:36-46

STEP 1

Up for Grabs

OPTIONS

Below, students compete in an eating contest that illustrates the importance of having teammates: 5-10 minutes.
Or, choose one of the option categories in the sidebar and see pages 73-77 for more "Getting Started" options.

Supplies needed: two paper bags with approximately six identical food items in each bag. Suggested food items are a hard-boiled egg, a small jar of baby food, an onion, licorice, a warm can of cola, and a container of yogurt.

Begin the lesson by asking: **Is anyone hungry today?** Choose two hungry volunteers—for best results choose one guy and one girl. Give them each a bag of food and explain that the goal of the game is to see which student can eat all of the food in his or her bag first.

Encourage the audience to cheer for the contestants. After one of the students has finished his or her second food item, point to the student who is losing and explain: **I think [name of the student who is behind] needs some help.** Ask for two other volunteers in the audience who are the same gender as the student who is falling behind. They should help by grabbing and eating their own food items out of the losing student's bag. Inevitably, this team of three people will end up beating the one student who remains alone in the game. Let the student who was at first winning express his or her displeasure about how unfair the contest was. Tell him or her it was all for the sake of making a point and thank the contestant for being a good sport. Let the winning team express what it was like to get to work as a team.

It's easier to do most things when somebody helps us. So why don't we ask for help more often?

Do you think your friends think more of you or less of you when you ask for help?

What kind of friendships would you have if you never asked for help or never let your friends help you?

STEP 2

Stories from the Front Lines

Below, read a story that introduces the "fox-hole" concept and will you help define Fox-Hole Friendship: 10-15 minutes.
Or, choose one of the option categories highlighted in the sidebar and see pages 73-77 for more "Getting Thirsty" options.

Supplies needed: copies of Resource 7, "Stories from the Front Lines" (page 67).

Pass out copies of Resource 7. Ask for a few volunteers to take turns reading the story aloud.

Many veterans of foreign wars seem to have a strong bond with the people they fought with on the front lines. Why do you think that is?

When two friends have an important purpose for their friendship and they "fight" for that purpose side by side, it can create the kind of bond we call a Fox-Hole Friendship. Besides friendships between veterans who fought together, where else do you tend to see close, "fox-hole" kinds of friendships?

Do you ever see Fox-Hole Friendships between Christians? Do you know of any examples?

Are most Christian friendships more like couch potato friendships or Fox-Hole Friendships? Why? What are yours like?

OPTIONS

STEP 3

Freeze Frame

OPTIONS

SMALL GROUP

SHORT MEETING TIME

JR. HIGH / HIGH SCHOOL COMBINED

SIXTH GRADE

Below, students make "freeze frame" pictures that depict how Jesus held the disciples accountable at Gethsemane.
Or, choose one of the option categories listed in the sidebar and see pages 73-77 for more "Getting the Word" options.

Supplies needed: Bibles, posterboard, pens.

Introduce the Scripture reading by saying: **Many Christians suffer from "Do-It-Yourself Syndrome." This syndrome is often marked by thoughts like: *I'm not doing well spiritually, but I can't tell anyone what I'm struggling with because then they'd know I'm not a perfect Christian.* Or, on the flip-side: *I know my friend is struggling spiritually but I can't say anything because I might make him upset.* The Do-It-Yourself Syndrome is one of the biggest obstacles we face if we want to build Fox-Hole Friendships. What would Jesus say about the Do-It-Yourself Syndrome? Let's find out.**

Divide into four teams. Assign each group one of the Scripture passages below. Have each group create "Freeze Frame" pictures for its passage. To make "Freeze Frame" pictures, students become characters or inanimate objects in the story, frozen in a portrayal of what happened in their scene. One person in each group should be the narrator and explain the pictures.

Assign these passages:
Scene 1: Matthew 26:36-39
Scene 2: Matthew 26:40-41
Scene 3: Matthew 26:42-44
Scene 4: Matthew 26:45-46

Jesus was going through one of His toughest times while He was here on earth. He knew He was going to die. He knew very soon He would be hung from a cross. In that critical time for Him, why do you think He wanted His friends to join Him in prayer?

Explain that Jesus had an "inner circle" of disciples, people He taught and included in more ways than the others. It was these three "inner circle" disciples—Peter, James, and John—whom Jesus asked to pray with Him.

Part of being a Fox-Hole Friend is keeping others accountable, or on track spiritually. That's why, when Jesus found His disciples sleeping, He woke them and asked them to continue praying. But the disciples were already tired and were unable to stay awake.

Note what Jesus said to His disciples when He found them sleeping. He asked them tough questions like, "Can't you pray with me?" and "Are you still sleeping?"

These questions are called "accountability" questions. Jesus asked tough questions of His disciples because He wanted to keep them "on track" in their commitments.

Did anyone catch the mind-blowing idea about accountability in this passage? Jesus wanted to have His Fox-Hole Friends with Him during this tough time in the garden. He kept them accountable to what He asked them to do and asked for their support. During tough times, even Jesus didn't want to do it alone.

BIBLE BYTES

Jesus at the Garden of Gethsemane

John 14:31-56

✱ BACKGROUND BYTES: It's important to note that the disciples had already made an extreme commitment to Jesus. By nature of being "disciples," they had committed to following Jesus and obeying Him completely. By asking tough questions like, "Can't you pray with me for one hour?" Jesus was keeping the disciples accountable to a commitment they had *already* made.

✱ SCRIPTURE BYTES: The Bible includes many stories of Fox-Hole Friends who served the Lord together on the front lines. See the stories of: David and Jonathan (1 Samuel 20:1-4ff.), Ruth and Naomi (Ruth 1:1-18), and Paul and Barnabas (Act 9:19-28ff.)

✱ BYTE-SIZE INSIGHTS: It's difficult and lonely to try to "do it yourself" as a Christian. But God doesn't ask us to do it on our own. In addition to the fact that we can ask for God's help, God is also faithful to provide us with partners, or Fox-Hole Friends, when we ask.

STEP 4

How to Be Fox-Hole Friends

OPTIONS

Below, small groups act out the best way to be Fox-Hole Friends to one another in tempting situations.
Or, choose one of the option categories in the sidebar and see pages 73-77 for more "Getting the Point" options.

Introduce the small group activity by saying: **Jesus is our model for friendship. He taught us that it's important to have Fox-Hole Friends. He also taught us what Fox-Hole Friends do. First, they make themselves accountable to one another. They have a commitment to listen to each other and to keep working together at growing closer to Jesus. Second, they keep each other accountable. That means they ask each other tough questions because they care and want their friends to do the right thing.**

Divide into small groups of six to eight students. Have each group come up with a skit that illustrates how one Fox-Hole Friend could keep another accountable. They should show a real-life situation that would cause one of the friends to struggle in his or her walk with Christ. Then have a friend or a group of friends do something to help that person stay on track.

If groups are stuck coming up with situations, here are two ideas to prime the pump: a friend is getting busy with school and sports and is deciding not to spend time with God; or, a friend made the cheerleading squad and now she's been attending many of the "popular" kids' parties where she's starting to drink and smoke.

You may want to circulate among the groups to make sure they understand the assignment and are making progress in it.

After 10 minutes, ask the groups to reassemble. One at a time, have each group act out its skit.

STEP 5

Accountability in Action

Below, students interview two real-life Fox-Hole Friends and take home a Fox-Hole Friendship Certificate.
Or, choose one of the option categories highlighted in the right sidebar and see pages 73-77 for more "Getting Personal" options.

Supplies needed: copies of Resource 8, "Tough Questions" (page 69), and copies of Resource 9, "Fox-Hole Friendship Certificate" (page 71), pens.
Set up: Ahead of time, ask one of your adult volunteers, another adult from your church, or a Foxhole Friend of your own (see Teacher Tip below) to share what accountability looks like. If possible, invite both partners in the accountability friendship to come and share with your students. In advance, write out the following questions and distribute them to a few students so that they can ask questions of these Foxhole Friends: **How did your Foxhole Friendship start? What are the toughest parts of being a Foxhole Friend? Are you ever scared to ask your friend tough accountability questions? What is the best part of having a Foxhole Friend?**

After the interview, pass out copies of Resource 8. Tell students to circle one of the tough questions they want to be asked or write their own. Explain that if students are ready to hold each other accountable, they should find a partner this week. Both partners should sign and date the Certificate (Resource 9). Encourage them to post the Certificate on their bathroom mirror or closet as a daily reminder of their commitment to Foxhole Friendship. Remind students that they can be Foxhole Friends with more than just one person.

Close in prayer, thanking God for giving us friends who climb into the Fox-Holes of life with us.

Teacher Tip: It may seem scary at first to invite one of your own accountability friends to speak, but the risk you take in opening up part of your own life to the group will encourage your students to do the same in their own lives.

OPTIONS

EXTRA ACTION
SMALL GROUP
FELLOWSHIP & WORSHIP
MOSTLY GUYS
EXTRA FUN
JR. HIGH HIGH SCHOOL COMBINED

On the Front Lines

I didn't know how to handle war.

Now my hands were shaking furiously. My stomach was pulling, twisting. I couldn't do anything to stop it. I panicked. I flat out panicked. I blew my cover and stood straight up. Like a man gone stark raving mad, I shot a few rounds straight into the sky. In a matter of seconds, bullets from the brush whizzed by my left and right. Another land mine exploded in the distance. I was a sitting duck.

Stuff happens in war. People flip out.

I think Mitch must have flipped out, too, to do what he did. I was a scared, out-of-place 19 year-old. I wasn't the kind of guy someone like Mitch would risk his life for. But he did. He jumped right up without thinking. He tackled me. I fought him like a cornered dog. I didn't know what I was doing. Mitch dragged me kicking and screaming back into the foxhole.

We didn't talk much in the fox hole. I was a wreck. I was cold, shaky, scared to death. We just sat there, silent. He gave me his coat. He fed me his rations.

It must have been hours—it felt like days—that we sat there in the fox-hole. A fox-hole was a hole you dug out to hide in. Soldiers like us who fought on the front lines had to dig a lot of fox-holes. Sometimes you had just minutes to dig a hole because there was no place else to hide for cover. Mitch saved my life when he pulled me into the fox hole.

I'm grateful for that day, that moment, when Mitch saved my life. Most often it's when I look at my children. You see, I've got a wife and three kids. So I guess I'm pretty normal, huh? But I'll never forget my Fox-Hole Friend. Each day I try to live with a little more courage because of him.

Tough Questions

Circle the question that you most need to be asked to be held accountable during the next month because of the struggles that you are having right now.

How are you treating your brother or sister?

Are you obeying and honoring your parents or step-parents?

Are you completing your homework on time and honestly?

Are you gossiping about other people?

How is your friendship with Jesus these days?

Are you reading your Bible as much as you'd like?

Are you remembering to pray for others?

Are you honoring God with what you watch on TV and at the movies?

Are you honoring God with the language you use? (Are you using swear words often?)

Are you taking advantage of opportunities to introduce others to Jesus?

Other: ____

Fox-Hole Friendship Certificate

On this ____ day of ____________, ______, ____________________

and ______________________________ commit to a Fox-Hole Friendship. We will:

1. Ask each other tough questions.
2. Support each other in our walks with God.
3. Never, never, never give up on our friendship.

______________________________ Your Signature

______________________________ Your Fox-Hole Friend's Signature

______________________________ Parent/Guardian or Other Signature

______________________________ Youth Worker's Signature

EXTRA ACTION

Step 1 - Electric Fence
Students help each other over a "fence."

Before students arrive, tape a large piece of crepe paper shoulder high across a doorway. Everyone must make it over the "electric fence" (represented by the crepe paper). They can not go under, around, or touch the crepe paper. Once a person is over the fence, he or she may not return to the original side until all students make it across safely. Students will have to work together and think strategically to be successful. Give as little direction as possible. Discuss questions like: **Did anyone try to make it over alone? What was that like? How did this task require everyone to work together? What are some things that make it hard to work together in life? Why do you think we don't work together more often?** *(Needed: crepe paper, tape.)*

Step 5 - Two-Man Chance Dive
Fox-Hole Friends take a trust dive together.

Since a Fox-Hole Friendship is based on trust, let students symbolize this by participating in a modified trust fall. Each partner needs a group of eight people to "spot" his or her jump—four on the left and four on the right. The spotters stand facing each other with their arms extended while holding the spotter's wrists across from them. Have partners stand side by side, facing the spotters. Spotters should bend at one knee slightly. Have an adult spot the faller's head. Stress safety. Go through a number of practice runs. Jump from a safe distance; for most groups, falling from a chair will be high enough. Fallers should cross their arms over their chest. Before falling, fallers should shout "Falling!" and wait to hear the spotters yell back, "Fall on!" Before they jump together, have partners explain to the group what they are trusting each other for as Fox-Hole Friends. *(Needed: chairs.)*

SMALL GROUP

Step 1 - Rock Climb Field Trip
Rock climb, rappel, or visit a ropes course.

Try meeting at an indoor rock climbing gym or a ropes course for the day. Or, if you really feel adventurous, arrange to go rappelling outdoors with an organization that provides equipment and guides. These activities teach more about "accountability" and trust than you ever can in a classroom. After the activity, debrief students about any lessons they learned about trusting, depending on, and challenging each other. Finish the meeting at the off-site location, if possible. *(Needed: special arrangements for an off-site field trip.)*

Step 3 - Living Readings
Assign each person a role to act out.

You may not have enough students to make three different "Freeze Frames." Instead, assign each of your students to a specific role in the story—Jesus, Peter, James, John, and other disciples as needed. After reading each scene, pause and have students act out a more detailed conversation that might have taken place between the characters. Interview the characters about what they are thinking and feeling. Use the discussion questions at the end of Step 3. *(Needed: Bibles.)*

Step 5 - Fox-Hole Team
Commit to being a Foxhole Team.

If you want to take your small group to the next level, ask students to make "foxhole" commitments to the entire group. Then spend some time practicing what that means—have each student share with the group what tough question from Resource 8 he or she wants group members to ask him or her consistently. Have students sign the "Fox-Hole Friendship Certificate" of other group members. *(Needed: copies of Resources 8 and 9.)*

LARGE GROUP

Step 1 - Key Grab
Two teams race to grab a set of keys.

Divide into two large teams with an equal number of students on each team. Have the two teams face each other while sitting down in long, single-file lines. Each team should hold hands all the way down the line and they must look straight across at the other team the entire time. (If they look any other direction, award the other team a point.) At one end of the two lines, place a chair with a set of keys on it. Stand at the front of the line and hold the hands of the first two people in line. Squeeze one of the leader's hands. That leader should then squeeze the hand of the person next to him or her. That hand squeeze should be passed all the way down the line to the person next to the keys, who should pick them up. No sounds are to to be made at all! This is a great teamwork test. You'll find that the signal will get dropped in some lines and get falsely started in lines where it doesn't really exist. Teams earn one point for correctly grabbing the keys, and lose one point for incorrectly grabbing the keys. Play several rounds. *(Needed: keys or other small object.)*

OPTIONS

SESSION FOUR

STEP 2 - VETERAN INTERVIEWS
Interview friends who fought in a war.

If possible, don't just tell a story—interview actual veterans who fought together on the front lines. For best results, have the veterans come to your class or you could videotape the interviews ahead of time and play them back for your group. One other variation: If you can't find two veterans who fought together, interview one and have him or her tell stories of the people he or she fought with. Make sure your interviewee(s) cover such topics as: what a foxhole is, the depth of friendship that's built while fighting on the front lines together, and the best and worst parts of fighting together. If you use this option, for the sake of variety don't use friendship interviews again in Step 4. *(Needed: guest interviewee(s); or interviews on videotape, TV, VCR.)*

STEP 4 - GET REAL
Tell about your need for accountability.

A lot of church kids are tired of hearing adults talk about being real but not modeling it. Surprise them with your honesty. Open up about a real problem you have. Forget generalities here. You need to be specific! Set up an accountability agreement with your group. Be willing to let them ask you how you're doing with your problem (as they agree to let you ask them about theirs). One youthworker had his group help him lose weight. He started each Sunday morning with a step on the scale. Do not cross appropriate boundaries between adults and students, but be as honest as you can.

STEP 1 - HUMAN MACHINES
Groups create "human machines."

Use this activity to introduce not only Fox-Hole Friendship, but also to teach an important lesson about the body of Christ. Divide into groups of six to eight students each and challenge each group to create a "human machine"—a machine must have various parts that move and work together. Groups can become anything from pinball machines to car engines. Give a prize to the most creative machine. Point out the way that everyone on each machine must do his or her unique and important job for the machine to function. Explain that this is how the body of Christ works, too—we each have different and unique things to add to each other; we must work together. *[Needed: prize (optional.)]*

STEP 2 - IT'S YOUR CALL
Decide to either tell the truth or suffer consequences in situations below.

Many teens, especially those who haven't grown up in the church, mistake confronting others as judging them. Write the situations below on newsprint or white board:
1. You're watching your Dad change the tire on his car and you notice he forgot to put on one of the bolts. 2. You're walking to school with your best friend and he starts to gossip about another student.
3. Your friend asks if she can copy your homework because she couldn't do hers since her little brother was sick and she had to help take care of him. 4. Your friend tells you he's going to a party tonight and he's planning on trying drugs. For each situation, discuss: **What would you say or do? Why? Would you be judging or confronting the person? What's the difference?** *(Needed: newsprint or white board, marker.)*

STEP 2 - FRIENDSHIP FEST
Celebrate Fox-Hole Friends in your group.

As youth leader, you probably know of at least one or two Fox-Hole Friendships that already exist among your students—where students are committed to keeping each other accountable and supporting each other on the front lines of following God. Celebrate these friendships. Tell stories you know that make good examples of Fox-Hole Friends. Let students talk about their friendships with one another. Let any student who wants to share statements like, "I am thankful for my friend ______, because he/she. . . ." *(Needed: various gifts and/or awards.)*

STEP 5 - PRAYER AND PRAISE
Worship and build community by singing and having a focused prayer time.

This option works best if students already have "Fox-Hole Friend" commitments to one another; or, allow time to choose Fox-Hole Friends during the lesson. Close your meeting by having your students sit on the floor with their partners. Take five minutes to sing some praise and worship songs, then have your students pray for one another in the areas they requested accountability. *(Needed: worship music.)*

OPTIONS

SESSION FOUR

Step 1 - Bracelet Race

Race to make friendship bracelets.

Use the "Up for Grabs" rules, but instead of an eating contest, have girls race to make friendship bracelets. *(Needed: strips of leather, beads, yarn.)*

Step 2 - Should I?

Cut tempting situations out of magazines.

Some girls may not relate to the military-based "fox-hole" theme. Instead you may want to refer throughout to Accountability Partners instead of Fox-Hole Friends. Instead of reading the fox-hole story, pass out old magazines. Tell girls to clip out articles and pictures that remind them of something they know they're not supposed to do but might like to do. Discuss: **How would you feel if you had a friend who helped you avoid some of these tempting things? A friend who sticks by you and helps you avoid tempting situations is called an Accountability Partner. Do you have an Accountability Partner? Do you want one?** *(Needed: magazines, scissors.)*

Step 4 - Mail Service

Write "Dear Accountability Partner" letters.

Most teen girls are willing to share their struggles and fears openly with others. This activity will help them do that. Pass out paper and pens; ask students to pretend someone in the class is their Accountability Partner. Give girls four minutes to write an anonymous "Dear Accountability Partner" letter listing areas they're struggling with and asking for advice and accountability. Collect the letters, mix them up, and redistribute them to the class. Now give students four minutes to write advice, encouragement and/or Scriptural help on the letter they've received. Return letters to the original owners but be sensitive to the students who want to remain anonymous. *(Needed: paper, pens.)*

Step 1 - Skirmish

Pairs of students race from "fox-hole" to "fox-hole" while dodging water balloons.

This game will get your guys excited and ready to learn about Fox-Hole Friends. Set up a course that includes a starting line, a finish line, and a number of "fox-holes." In war, fox-holes are places soldiers hide for protection. So, in this situation a fox-hole could be an overturned table, a refrigerator box guys can crawl in, or anything else you can think of. Have two guys race through the course at a time. Arm all other guys with water balloons and set them up along the outside of the course. See which pair gets through the course fastest and "bombed" with water balloons the fewest times. If you're playing this game in a gym instead of outside, use tennis balls; if you're playing in a classroom, you can use paper wads. Use this game to introduce what "fox-holes" are. *(Needed: water balloons, tennis balls, or paper wads; tables, boxes, or other supplies to make "fox-holes.")*

Step 5 - Altar Building

Build altars out of stones to remind students of their friendship commitments.

Give each guy a rock and a marker. Have guys write their names on their rocks. Then pass the rocks around the circle and have each guy initial everyone else's rock. Then take the guys to a place where you can build your altar. This could be outside in some woods nearby or it could be in the building. Your location should be a place where the rocks won't be seen or disturbed. One at a time, have the guys place their rocks in a pile. As they do this, each guy needs to say one way that he needs the rest of the group to hold him accountable. When you are done, you will have a little "altar" to remember your commitments by. *(Needed: rocks, markers.)*

Step 1 - Teamwork Fest

Participate in a number of team games.

Try some of these teamwork games or make up your own:

- **Stand Up:** Groups of three sit on the ground with their backs together, and try to stand up without using their hands at all.
- **Handicapped Obstacle:** Assign various handicaps to group members (no sight, one leg, no arms, no speaking). Then have them complete a simple obstacle course together—no time limit, just teamwork.
- **Beam Pass:** Have students stand on a beam or log with both halves of the line facing the middle. Everyone must get to the opposite-side position without stepping off.
- **Few Feet:** Challenge your group to see how few feet they can have touching the ground (total of the group).

(Needed: variable.)

Step 5 - Up for Grabs II

Play "Up for Grabs" in teams.

If your students are ready, help them get into Fox-Hole Groups—groups of friends who make accountability commitments to one another. Leave a few minutes for them to sign one another's Foxhole Friendship Certificates. Then give the new Foxhole Groups a chance to compete together. This will help close the meeting on an upbeat note. Review the rules for "Up for Grabs" in Step 1. Give each team a bag filled with the same 6-10 food and drink items. (It would be best if these are different items than the ones you used in Step 1!) See which team can eat all the items first. Give the team that wins a jar of baby food for a prize. *[Needed: food items (see list for Step 1), prizes.]*

OPTIONS

S E S S I O N   F O U R

MEDIA

STEP 1 - FRIEND IN YOU

Put clips of students and their friends to the song "You've Got a Friend in Me."

For a shorter opening try the following video opening. Take your video camera to a couple of local schools right before classes let out. After asking permission from the administration, shoot short clips of kids together: groups by the locker, walking through the halls, playing basketball, holding hands, talking to a teacher. Make sure each shot is less than five seconds, with the total footage less than three minutes. If you keep the shots short, you won't have to spend time editing the piece. When you play the video for the students, play the theme song from the movie *Toy Story* in the background ("You've Got a Friend in Me"). *(Needed: TV, VCR, pre-made home video, CD player, CD recording of "You've Got a Friend in Me.")*

STEP 2 - FOXHOLE MEDIA

Use video, magazine pictures, books, or other media to explain "Fox-Hole Friends."

Look for ways to use additional media to introduce your discussion of "Fox-Hole Friendship." For example:

- Show clips from old war movies of soldiers fighting in fox-holes (screen them for appropriateness for your group).
- Show a clip from a documentary of "Desert Storm" (the war against Iraq) where military leaders discuss the strategic importance of fox-holes.
- Bring in a magazine like LIFE from the World War II era, or a book with pictures of soldiers fighting in fox-holes.

The goal for this activity is to get them thinking: **What would it be like in a fox-hole? Who would I want in *my* fox-hole?** *(Needed: various media.)*

SHORT MEETING TIME

STEP 1 - GRAB AS YOU GO

Play "Up for Grabs" as students arrive.

Instead of waiting for everyone to arrive, start playing "Up for Grabs" when the first guy and girl arrive. As others arrive, girls should jump in to help the girls team, and guys jump in to help the guys. Instead of a long discussion, have students discuss with one or two people next to them: **If we can get more done when we work together, why don't we ask for help more often?** *(Needed: see Step 1.)*

STEP 2 - YOUR STORY

Replace discussion with a short talk.

After reading Resource 7, tell a story about one of your own friendships. Use it as an example of what it means to have a Fox-Hole Friendship that involves keeping a friend accountable as you both live the "front lines" of following God. *(Needed: see Step 2.)*

STEP 3 - JERUSALEM JOURNAL

Write newspaper stories about Scripture.

Instead of making "living collages," have your three small groups each write a short newspaper account of the scene you assign them. Use the questions at the end of Step 3. *(Needed: paper, pencils.)*

STEPS 4/5 - SHORT STORIES

Arrange for students or adults to give testimonies of their Fox-Hole Friendships.

You can accomplish the goals for both Steps 4 and 5 with one set of student or adult testimonies. Tell your speakers to get very specific about their friendship, including actual situations that involved asking each other tough, confronting questions. Also, allow your speakers an opportunity to encourage the rest of the group to be accountable. In closing, pass out copies of Resources 8 and 9 for students to complete at home. *(Needed: guest speakers.)*

URBAN

STEP 2 - FRONT-LINE FRIENDS

Groups imagine they are reporters on the "front lines" of serious action.

Urban groups may not relate as well to the "fox-hole"/war imagery. Instead introduce the concept of being on the "front lines" in a way they can relate to with this simulation activity. Break into three teams and announce that teams are television reporters for the city's Christian TV station—WGOD. Each team was covering a routine story when a city-wide riot broke out. Each team must give two TV reports, one as if during the crisis and the other reporting how they got out safely by depending on God and working together as friends on the front lines.

- TEAM 1 was en route to the station when it got caught in gang cross-fire. It is now reporting from between two trucks. The gangs are closing in on the reporters' location.
- TEAM 2 has been kidnapped by four armed bank robbers. The thieves have allowed Team 2 to report their demands, but they have threatened to detonate a bomb and destroy millions of dollars in property if they do not get $1 million in one hour.
- TEAM 3 is doing a story from the city's highest security prison. There's been a prisoner uprising. The team and the guards are confined in cells. The team is reporting the demands from Cell Block 4. The prisoners are threatening to kill one cell block group per hour.

STEP 4 - FOX-HOLE ADD-ONS

Use these situations with an urban twist to help students come up with their own.

If groups get stuck coming up with ideas for the temptation situations in Step 4, here are two ideas with urban twists:

(1) Fyseen has sworn to wait for sex until marriage, but now he's telling you he's been getting hot and heavy with Rasheeda.

(2) Han-Min wants to get rid of her Christian CDs because she's into only Gangsta Rap now. *(Needed: see Step 4.)*

JR. HIGH / HIGH SCHOOL COMBINED

STEP 3 - IN THE GARDEN

Use more questions, a trip to a "garden," and music to draw students into the Bible.

Find a quiet, relaxing place outside or a special place in your church or home where your group can "get away." Before moving to this "garden," discuss: **Have you ever faced a really tough morning when you knew your day would be difficult?** (First day at a new school, parents' divorce, funeral, etc.) Help students understand that Jesus was facing an excruciatingly tough day—He knew He was going to die. Move to the "garden" area. Read Matthew 26:36-46. In addition to the questions and comments in Step 3, discuss: **Did Jesus' friends do a good job supporting Him? When you've been through tough times, were your friends there for you? What did they do?** Finally, give students time to think about what they've read while you play a song in the background. *(Needed: The Big Picture CD, CD player.)*

STEP 5 - MORE TOUGH QUESTIONS

Encourage same-age partners and add high school-level questions to Resource 8.

Logistically, this step will work better for future follow-up if the partners attend the same school and if the partners are similar in life stage and corresponding temptations. Make this clear in your instructions and encourage middle school students to choose middle school partners and senior highers to choose senior high partners. Before you copy Resource 8 and distribute it to your students, you may also want to add questions such as: **Are you driving in a responsible manner? Are you honoring the curfew your parents have established for you? Are you drinking or using drugs?** *(Needed: see Step 5.)*

SIXTH GRADE

STEP 1 - TOUCH TAG

Play a tag game that involves team work.

Many sixth graders would rather be an active participant instead of an observer. "Touch Tag" will keep them active. Choose two volunteers to be IT and IT 2. Explain that each person tagged by IT becomes part of IT—they must hold IT's hand, then use his or her free hand to tag others. Explain that anyone tagged by IT 2 also becomes a part of IT 2, but should hold to some part of IT 2's clothing with both hands and *not* tag others. Play until everyone has been tagged. Discuss: **Which team had the biggest advantage? Why? Is it easier to do things with help or on your own? Why? What are some examples? Is following God easier to do on your own or with someone else's help?**

STEP 2 - ACCOUNTABILITY GAME

Unscramble the word "accountability."

Sixth graders may need a special introduction to the big word "accountability." Divide into three teams. Give each team a pile of cut-out letters that spell accountability. See which team can unscramble the word first. **What is accountability?** Supplement answers with this info: **It means holding someone responsible for his or her actions. For example, if my friend and I want to keep each other accountable to stop swearing, we could charge one another a quarter every time we catch each other saying a swear word. How else can we keep each other accountable?** *(Needed: paper, pen or marker, scissors.)*

STEP 3 - BIBLE COMIC BOOK

Draw comic frames of the Bible story.

Instead of making "living collages," pass out markers and paper and have students draw the Bible story in a series of comic book frames. Divide into four groups and assign each group to draw one scene. Use the discussion questions at the end of Step 3.

PLANNING CHECKLIST

STEP 1 (5-10 MINUTES, UNLESS NOTED)

- ❒ **Extra Action:** Electric Fence (10-15 min.)
- ❒ **Small Group:** Rock Climb Field Trip (Extra time required)
- ❒ **Large Group:** Key Grab
- ❒ **Little Bible:** Human Machines
- ❒ **Mostly Girls:** Bracelet Race
- ❒ **Mostly Guys:** Skirmish (10-15 min.)
- ❒ **Extra Fun:** Teamwork Fest (10-20 min.)
- ❒ **Media:** Friend in You (5 min.)
- ❒ **Short Time:** Grab as You Go (3-5 min.)
- ❒ **Sixth Grade:** Touch Tag

STEP 2 (10-15 MINUTES, UNLESS NOTED)

- ❒ **Heard It All Before:** Veteran Interviews
- ❒ **Little Bible:** It's Your Call
- ❒ **Fellowship & Worship:** Friendship Fest
- ❒ **Mostly Girls:** Should I?
- ❒ **Media:** Foxhole Media
- ❒ **Short Time:** Your Story (5-10 min.)
- ❒ **Urban:** Front-Line Friends
- ❒ **Sixth Grade:** Accountability Game

STEP 3 (15-20 MINUTES, UNLESS NOTED)

- ❒ **Small Group:** Living Readings
- ❒ **Short Time:** Jerusalem Journal (10-15 min.)
- ❒ **Combined:** In the Garden
- ❒ **Sixth Grade:** Bible Comic Book

STEP 4 (10-15 MINUTES, UNLESS NOTED)

- ❒ **Heard It All Before:** Get Real
- ❒ **Mostly Girls:** Mail Service
- ❒ **Short Time:** Short Stories* (10 min.)
- ❒ **Urban:** Fox-Hole Add-Ons

STEP 5 (5-10 MINUTES, UNLESS NOTED)

- ❒ **Extra Action:** Two-Man Chance Dive
- ❒ **Small Group:** Fox-Hole Team
- ❒ **Fellowship & Worship:** Prayer and Praise
- ❒ **Mostly Guys:** Altar Building
- ❒ **Extra Fun:** Up For Grabs II
- ❒ **Combined:** More Tough Questions

**combined steps*

SESSION

5

Stretcher Friends

YOUR GOALS FOR THIS SESSION:

Choose one or more

☐ To help students learn how four friends found a creative way to introduce their paralyzed friend to Jesus.

☐ To help students understand a mind-blowing idea about introducing Jesus: Jesus can meet your friends' needs.

☐ To help students become Stretcher Friends—friends that find creative ways to introduce the people in their lives to Jesus

☐ Other: ____

____

Your Bible Base

Mark 2:1-5, 12

STEP 1

Human Stretcher

Below, teams race "human stretchers" across the room by carrying a team member by his or her wrists and ankles.
Or, choose one of the option categories listed in the sidebar and see pages 89-93 for more "Getting Together" options.

OPTIONS

Supplies needed: colored candies.

Instead of just saying "Get into groups of three!" use this creative way to break into small groups. Hand out one candy to each student. Explain that students should put the candy on their tongues but leave their mouths open and then find four other people who have the same color candy and sit down as a team. For best results, ahead of time organize your candies into multiples of four per color. NOTE: If your group won't divide equally into groups of five, you will have some students "left over" after this mixer. Allow them to join whatever team of five they want.

Introduce the game "Human Stretcher" by saying: **Has anyone ever been carried on a stretcher? When?** Pause for responses, then continue: **Has anyone ever actually been part of a stretcher? I didn't think so. Well, today you're going to have a chance to be part of a human stretcher.**

Designate the smallest member of each team the "stretcher." The other four or five students are the stretcher bearers. Two students should grab one ankle and two students should grab one arm. Let students practice carrying the "stretcher" around the room. Then, line the teams up and let them race from one side of your room to the other. Declare a winner.

Congratulate teams on their great job being human stretchers. Then say: **There's another way we can be "human stretchers" to our friends. Many of our friends don't know Jesus. When we bring our friends to Jesus we are like human stretchers.**

STEP 2

The Closet Jesus Fan

Below, students interview another group member and introduce him or her to the rest of the group. Then, one student acting like a "Closet Jesus Fan" attempts to introduce the rest of the group to Jesus: 10-15 minutes.
Or, choose one of the option categories listed on the sidebar and see pages 89-93 for more "Getting Thirsty" options.

OPTIONS

Set up: Ahead of time, prepare one student to roleplay the part of a Closet Jesus Fan in a mock interview you will conduct. A Closet Jesus Fan is someone who is afraid of telling others about Jesus. Instruct your actor to act according to certain guidelines during the interview. He or she should avoid mentioning anything about being a Christian, going to church, or knowing Jesus; act shy and nervous; speak only in vague terms about being a Christian; and keep trying to change the subject to something less challenging like lunch, a recent movie, or homework.

Tell students to find partners. Explain that they are going to practice introducing each other before you talk about introducing Jesus. Students have three minutes to learn as much about their partners as they can by asking questions such as: *Where were you born? What's your favorite restaurant? What do you like best about your brothers and sisters?* Explain that each student will use this information to make a brief introduction of his or her partner.

After three minutes, give each student a chance to introduce his or her partner by sharing three things he or she learned from the interview.

Say: **Sometimes it's hard to know how to introduce our friends. And it can be even harder to introduce our friends to Jesus. I've asked [name of the student actor you've prepared] to come and show us what it might be like to introduce Jesus.**

Interview your student actor with the questions like:

- **So, do you go to church?**
- **Have you ever invited any of your friends to go to church with you?**
- **What do you think of Jesus?**
- **Do you want to tell the group anything about Jesus?**
- **Is there anything you particularly like about Jesus?**
- **You don't seem to be too excited about your faith in Jesus. Isn't Jesus supposed to be your best friend?**

After the interview, discuss: **How would you summarize the introduction style of this student?**

Did this person give Jesus an effective introduction? Why or why not?

It's probably obvious to you that this person was what we'll call a "Closet Jesus Fan." He was terrified of telling others about Jesus. He probably keeps his faith hidden, as if in a "closet." How many of you find it awkward or even scary to try to introduce Jesus?

What are some things someone might find scary about introducing Jesus?

Let's face it. None of us wants to introduce Jesus if it's going to make us look like a geek, right? The problem is our fear often keeps our faith locked up. Instead of being Stretcher Friends, we end up being Closet Jesus Fans. Today we're going to talk about how to introduce Jesus without looking like a geek.

STEP 3

Stretcher Friends Melodrama

Below, students act out a melodrama about four friends who introduce a paralyzed friend to Jesus: 15-20 minutes.
Or, choose one of the option categories in the sidebar and see pages 89-93 for more "Getting the Word" options.

Supplies needed: Resource 10, "Stretcher Friends Melodrama" (page 86), one candy bar or piece of candy per student.
Set up: Ahead of time, prepare a student to wait outside your room from a place where he or she can hear you without being seen. In the lesson below, you will say at one point, "You may not know it, but Jesus died for you because of how much He loves you." That will be your actor's cue. He or she should burst into the room and say, "They're giving away free candy bars outside. Come on! Hurry outside!" This simulation will help start a discussion about why we should introduce others to Jesus.

Before we study about how to introduce Jesus, let's talk a little about friendship. I'm wondering something. What do you think is the most extreme act of friendship someone could ever do? Take a few responses, then ask: **What about dying for a friend? Don't you think dying for someone is the greatest act of friendship? Has anyone ever died for you? You may not know it, but Jesus died for you because of how much He loves you.** *Student enters.*

At this point, your lesson may get a little chaotic. The student that you prepared ahead of time should burst in the room and yell, "They're giving away free candy outside. Come on! Hurry outside!" Some of your students may immediately get up and head outside. Others may stay, watching you for a cue. Go ahead and excuse your students to go outside and each get the candy. You may want to recruit an adult ahead of time to stand outside and distribute the candy.

Call your students back to the room. Explain: **Wasn't that great of (the student's name) to run in here and tell us about the free candy bars?**

Get back to the lesson by saying: **Dying for someone is the ultimate act of friendship. When Jesus died for us on the cross it was the greatest act of love, sacrifice, and friendship ever. But the second most extreme act of friendship is to introduce someone to Jesus. So many times we keep the good news of our friendship with Jesus to ourselves. Instead,**

OPTIONS

LITTLE BIBLE BACKGROUND

URBAN

JR. HIGH / HIGH SCHOOL COMBINED

we should be just like the student who burst into our classroom to tell us about the candy. Our news about Jesus is so much better than a candy bar, and yet we hesitate to introduce others to Him.

In a melodrama, volunteers act out the story as you read it. Give these directions: **We're about to read a melodrama. And while I want you to have fun with this, see if you can find a mind-blowing idea about friendship in this melodrama.** Assign nine of your most vocal, outgoing students to the roles listed on Resource 10. Other students who want to participate can be "People." Read Resource 10 and have your actors and audience act out the scene as you read.

How were the four friends in this story different than the Closet Jesus fan?

What would have happened to the paralyzed guy if the friends had done nothing?

Why do you think the four friends were so motivated to bring their friend to Jesus?

What can this story teach us about introducing Jesus to our friends?

Did anyone catch the mind-blowing idea about introducing Jesus? Like you and me, these four friends just might have been terrified about introducing Jesus. After all, their paralyzed friend could have rejected Jesus and refused His help, and the four guys could have looked like geeks. But get this: Those four friends understood that Jesus can meet your friends' needs. Jesus can heal your friends wherever they hurt. That's a mind-blowing idea about introducing Jesus, isn't it?

BIBLE BYTES

Introducing Others to Jesus

Mark 2:1-5, 12

✱ BACKGROUND BYTES: Many scholars believe that the scene of this Bible story is Andrew and Peter's house. • Many houses in Jerusalem had an outside staircase leading to a flat roof.

✱ SCRIPTURE BYTES: For other stories that involve Jesus meeting the needs of those who came to Him, see: Matthew 4:23-35; 8:1-4; 18-26; 27-31; and 15:21-28.

✱ BYTE-SIZE INSIGHTS: Many non-believers are "paralyzed" by their sin and lifestyle—they are unable to go to Jesus. Someone must bring them to Jesus. We can bring people like this to Jesus by praying, giving our testimony, inviting friends to church, etc.

STEP 4

How to Be Stretcher Friends

Below, three students perform monologues and all discuss how they could introduce the actors to Jesus: 10-15 minutes.
Or, choose one of the option categories in the sidebar and see pages 89-93 for more "Getting the Point" options.

Supplies needed: copies of Resource 11, "A Friend in Need . . ." (page 87), copies of Resource 12, "I Will Introduce You to Jesus" (page 88).
Set up: Ahead of time, assign three volunteers one of the monologues on Resource 11. Prepare them with a copy of Resource 11 and encourage them to practice so that they can read their lines as convincingly as possible on the day of your meeting. If you used Resource 2 in Step 4 of Session 2, these three characters will be familiar. For best results, choose the same actors from Session 2 to read their character's lines again here. This resource is a follow-up to Resource 2.

Introduce the monologue reading by saying: **It's one thing to admire what these four friends did and another thing to be Stretcher Friends in our own world. Sit back and listen now to the stories of three teens who have needs only Jesus can meet. Pay close attention because in a few minutes we'll discuss what it would mean to be a Stretcher Friend to these people.**

Have your actors perform their monologues.

Ask students to go and stand by one of the three characters that they would like to help introduce to Jesus. Groups don't have to be equal in size. If any group is larger than 4-5 students, break it into smaller groups as necessary. Pass out pens and copies of Resource 12. Each small group should brainstorm answers to the questions on the resource sheet as they relate to the character they've chosen. Give groups about 10 minutes to brainstorm answers. Then have one spokesperson per group present his or her small group's answers.

OPTIONS

STEP 5

Stretcher Friends in Action

OPTIONS

Below, students tape names of friends to a cross, symbolizing their commitment to pray for and introduce those friends to Jesus: 5-10 minutes. Or, choose one of the option categories in the sidebar and see pages 89-93 for more "Getting Personal" options.

Supplies needed: a wooden cross, or large branches and nails, or two pieces of wood and nails; tape, index cards, pens.
Set up: Bring in a large wooden cross and put it on one side of your room. You can make a wooden cross by nailing two large branches or pieces of wood together in the shape of a cross.

Your friends who don't know Jesus have needs that only Jesus can meet. Their lives could change if only someone would step up and introduce them to Jesus. We've spent some time today starting to answer the question "HOW do we introduce our friends to Jesus?" Now we need to decide WHO we can introduce to Jesus.

Give pens and an index card to each student. Ask students to indicate the person that they will try to introduce to Jesus on the card by writing his or her name, drawing a picture, or writing something that reminds them of him or her. On the back side of the card, ask them to write two specific actions that they will take to introduce their friend to Jesus. Encourage them to use some of the ideas that they shared when they discussed Resource 13. Or they can come up with their own ideas to be Stretcher Friends in action.

After three or four minutes, point to the cross at the side of your room. Ask students to come forward and tape their index cards to the cross**. Every time we look at this cross it will be a reminder of our commitments to introduce one friend to Jesus.** If possible, leave the cross where it is for the next few weeks as a reminder. Make sure you set an example by putting an index card on the cross with one of your own friend's names on it.

Finally, close in prayer. Ask God to provide your group with opportunities to be Stretcher Friends and introduce others to Jesus.

Stretcher Friends Melodrama

Characters:

Jesus	Frank (Friend #1)
The People	Fran (Friend #2)
The Stretcher	Fred (Friend #3)
Pete, the paralytic	Frieda (Friend #4)
Two roof shingles	

One day Jesus was walking along. He decided to enter a house. A bunch of people heard that Jesus was in the house, so they crowded in. In fact, it was so crowded that some of the people were sitting on top of one another. The people were on the edge of their seats. They "shushed" anyone who made any noise that kept them from hearing Jesus' preaching.

The four friends, Frank, Fran, Fred, and Freida, tiptoed up to the house so that they wouldn't disrupt Jesus' teaching. Peering inside, they saw how crowded it was. Well, all except Freida, who was so short that she had to climb on top of Fred's back to see inside. Frank, Fran, Fred, and Freida were very sad because they had really hoped that their friend Pete, who was paralyzed, could see Jesus so Jesus could heal Pete. But there were too many people. They were so sad that they couldn't even walk; they could only crawl away from the house.

Suddenly Fran jumped to her feet and yelled, "Wait. I have an idea."

"What?" yelled Frank.

However, Fran was partly deaf so she screamed louder, "What?" to Frank.

Frank returned the favor by yelling at the top of his lungs, "What?"

This time Fran heard him. She yelled, "We could go through the roof."

All four friends leaped for joy. They were still leaping for joy when Fred yelled, "Hey, we can bring Pete, our paralyzed friend with us." Still leaping for joy, all four friends yelled together, "What a great idea!"

They found a stretcher lying on the side of the road and picked it up. Then they found Pete, picked him up, and put him on the stretcher. They got lost on the way back to the house so they had to walk a little extra.

Finally they found the house. They pried up two of the roof shingles. Being very careful, they lowered the stretcher and Pete in front of Jesus. All four friends were smiling at Jesus. Jesus smiled big back at them. Jesus said to Pete, "Your sins are forgiven."

At that point, Pete got up off the stretcher and walked out of the house. He was so excited that he could walk, he hopped around a little. Then he jumped. Then he skipped around Jesus. Everyone in the house was shocked and gasped in unison. Together they said, "Praise God!" The four friends began leaping for joy again and giving each other high fives.

The end.

A Friend in Need . . .

Try to put yourself into the shoes of these students as you read their thoughts and feelings aloud.

Student #1: Clothes Carol

I feel like everyone is judging me every time I walk onto our school campus. If I could read their thoughts, they'd probably be thinking stuff like, "She's so out of style," or "Her clothes are so lame." Why do they judge me so much? And why do I even care that they judge me in the first place? Why is it so important to me that other people approve of how I look? I wish I didn't care so much, but I can't help it. I guess that I'll never have the clothes it takes to be accepted.

Student #2: New Girl Nancy

It's been a whole month at this school and I still feel like a loner. There was that other new girl who started having lunch with me, but pretty soon she joined the basketball team and made some new friends and ditched me. Now it's just me eating lunch alone again. I just hate sitting at that lunch table alone. I try to pretend as if I'm reading my English homework so that nobody will guess how alone I feel. I may be able to hide my loneliness from other people, but not myself.

Student #3: Failing Frank

I'm still not cutting it. I try in math, but the numbers just don't make sense. My other classes are OK, but not math. Even my older brother tried to help me, and he did help a bit, but not enough. I just wish I didn't have to take math. My parents are really getting mad at me. They say that I'm messing up my chances of going to a good college. But that feels so far away. All I care about is finishing this school year and passing my last math test.

I Will Introduce You to Jesus

I will **PRAY** for . . .

What kind of **NEEDS** could Jesus meet in your friend's life?

What are some **CREATIVE WAYS** you could introduce your friend to Jesus?

1. **I could . . .**

2. **I could . . .**

3. **I could . . .**

4. **I could . . .**

5. **I could . . .**

EXTRA ACTION

Step 1 - Hoop It Up

Race to see how fast students can get hula hoops to move around their circle.

Instruct the group to stand in a circle. Choose one person to be the "starter" and lay one hula hoop on the starter's right shoulder and the other on his or her left shoulder. Next, have students grab hands. On your signal, the group must race to get the hula hoops around the circle in opposite directions and back to the starter. They do this by stepping through the hoop, then darting their head through. They must keep their hands clasped together at all times. At some point the hoops will intersect, which will make things more interesting. Discuss: **Have you ever heard the saying "I had to jump through hoops for him"? What does it mean? Some of your friends may think they have to "jump through hoops" to know Jesus. But all they have to do is come to Jesus as they are. We're going to talk today about how to help our friends do just that!** *(Needed: two large hula hoops.)*

Step 5 - Shout Tag

A combination "tag" and sharing activity.

Junior high students are not always comfortable sharing important information. But if you get them involved in an active game, they just might start sharing before they even know it. Choose one person to be "It." Play like "Freeze Tag" (whenever It tags someone, he or she must stand "frozen") with this variation: to get "unfrozen" students must shout out their answers to this question: **What's the name of one unchurched friend you will pray for?** Each round, switch "Its" and questions. Other questions include: **What are you most afraid of about sharing your faith?** and **What's one lesson you learned today about sharing your faith?**

SMALL GROUP

Step 1 - Picture This!

Two options for starting discussion.

Here are two suggestions for getting more personal with your small group:

• School Trip: Take a field trip to one of the schools your students attend. Take a walk around the school and tell students to picture in their minds some of their friends who don't know Jesus.

• Yearbook Discussions: Gather recent yearbooks from your students' schools. As students enter, encourage them to thumb through the books. This is sure to stimulate plenty of "Look, there's so and so" kinds of comments. Ask as many questions as you can about who your students' friends are, what the various people are like, etc. This will get students thinking about specific people. After either of the activities, discuss: **Do you believe every person needs Jesus? Why or why not? Do the people at your schools need Jesus? Who might God want you to introduce to Jesus?**

(Needed: transportation or yearbooks.)

Step 4 - Testimonies

Practice giving personal testimonies.

One of the best ways to practically prepare students to share their faith is to help them write "testimonies." These are 1-2 minute personal stories about 1) What the subject's life was like before he or she knew Jesus; 2) How he or she became a Christian; and 3) What it means to "walk with God" and have a "relationship with God" in the subject's own words. Tell students to write out their testimonies in two or three paragraphs. Then ask for volunteers to give their testimonies to the class. Discuss the best ways they can share their testimonies with their friends. *(Needed: paper, pencils.)*

LARGE GROUP

Step 1 - Stretcher Races

Play "Human Stretcher" with team reps.

Capitalize on the *energy* of a large group. Divide into two or more affinity groups (guys vs. girls, 7th vs. 8th grade, etc.) Have each group send up five team representatives and have them race as instructed in Step 1. Encourage the audience to cheer loudly.

Step 2 - Life without Jesus?

Prepare actors to detail life without Jesus.

Sometimes the standard of expectations for drama performances is higher among teens in a large group. Instead of the "Closet Jesus Fan" skit, ask your drama team or two or three actors ahead of time to write and perform their own "life without Jesus" monologues. These should be stories that detail how life would be different if the actors didn't know Jesus. They should be written, however, in the present tense; for example: "My life looks good on the outside, but I'm missing something. I don't feel satisfied." At the end of the monologues, have the students write down three things that would be different in their own lives if they didn't know Jesus or three things that might change if they committed their lives to Christ for the first time. *(Needed: paper, pens.)*

Step 4 - Group Variation

Use Resources 11 & 12 in small groups.

Break down into small groups of sixto eight students each. Pass out one copy of Resource 11 to each group. Tell the groups to choose three people to read the parts of the three characters to the rest of the group. Then ask the group to choose one of the three characters to whom they'd like to be a Stretcher Friend. Ask one person in each group to be the "scribe" and record any ideas the group comes up with on Resource 12. Afterward, have the scribes share their answers with the rest of the class.

STEP 2 - EMT VISIT

Arrange for an EMT to talk to your class.

Call the local fire department and see if you can get an Emergency Medical Technician (EMT) to come visit for a short introduction about emergency response. Have the guest talk about what it's like to be on the scene of a life and death situation. Prepare students to ask questions like: **How does it feel to deal with people in crisis? What's the toughest accident you've ever dealt with? What's the most extravagant length you've ever gone for somebody else? Did you put yourself at risk to help someone else?** After the guest leaves, discuss: **How can we be like "EMTs" to our friends? What kinds of crises are your friends facing? Have you ever seen yourself as an EMT for Christ?** *(Needed: guest speaker.)*

STEP 5 - INTRODUCTION NIGHT

Hold a special event for students' friends.

If your students have "heard it all before," this is another opportunity to challenge them to start living it out. Use the time you have for Step 5 to introduce a special "Introduction Night"—an event your students can bring the unchurched friends and for whom they have committed to pray. Ask students to help you brainstorm an event that would help them effectively introduce Jesus to their friends.

Possibilities:

- A dinner at your house or the church.
- A fun activity—anything from a lock-in or "road rally" to a night at the movies.
- A special Sunday school or mid-week service with a special format that will help introduce unchurched students to Jesus.

You might prepare a few students to give their testimonies. Or you might give a short talk to help introduce Jesus. *(Needed: variable.)*

STEP 2 - THE GREATEST LOVE

Discuss great acts of love.

Some students in your group may not yet be spiritually mature enough to relate to the "Closet Jesus Fan" illustration. Instead, start by discussing: **What's the greatest act of love anyone's ever made for you?** Then, when you discuss the following questions, have students move to the left if they agree with the first choice, and to the right if they agree with the second choice. **Which do you think is a greater act of love: Someone climbing the highest mountain to be with the one he or she loves, or someone leaving, even though he or she doesn't want to, because it's the best thing to do for the one he or she loves? A son dying for his father, or a father dying to save his son?** Add as many other questions as you can. Then detail as best you can the ultimate act of love God made on our behalf—He sent His Son Jesus to die for our sins.

STEP 3 - LIVING WATER ANYONE?

Use John 4:4-26 as your Bible text.

Another Bible story for a group with little Bible background might be Jesus' encounter with the woman at the well. Read John 4:4-26. Use the "melodrama" idea in Step 3. You'll have to write a simple script yourself. Here are a few lines to get you started: **Most Jewish men hated Samaritan women. They held their noses up in the air when they saw one. They made disgusting, snobbish sounds. But when Jesus met a Samaritan woman, He went out of His way to serve her.** You can tie in the "Stretcher Friends" terminology in two ways: 1) Some students might need to get on the "stretcher" like the woman at the well did and come to God through Jesus for the first time. 2) Discuss how the Samaritan woman, once she experienced a relationship with God through Jesus, went on to be a Stretcher Friend to many other Samaritans by introducing them to Jesus. *(Needed: Bibles.)*

STEP 2 - SHOW & TELL

Find objects that represent lessons students have learned in the series.

Before getting too far in the lesson, take some time to review what students have been learning in the series. Ask students to walk around outside your meeting room (or provide a number of various, random objects if going outside is not possible). Tell students to find one object that summarizes a lesson they have learned about Jesus' friendship to them during this series. Have each student share and explain the object he or she found. Encourage students to share with an attitude of worship, thanking Him for serving us, valuing us, forgiving us, and modeling accountability for us. Lead your students through the following discussion: **Don't all these things make you glad that you know such a great God? Don't you wish everyone could experience God's forgiveness, friendship, and other great qualities? How can we share what we're learning with our friends?** *(Needed: random items).*

STEP 5 - PRAYER, NAIL, SONG

Pray, listen, and take home a reminder.

Make Step 5 more worshipful and reflective with these variations. First, while students are filling out their cards, play a recording of a challenging song like Al Denson's, "Be The One." (This song talks about accepting the call to share our faith with the world.) Second, as students tape the names of their friends on the cross as a commitment to share their faith, have a basketful of nails available at the foot of the cross. Encourage students to take a nail and keep it with them as a physical reminder to share their faith. Finally, have students pair up with a close friend and spend a few minutes praying for their friends who need to be introduced to Jesus. *(Needed: CD or cassette player, CD or cassette, nails, others supplies listed in Step 5.)*

MOSTLY GIRLS

Step 1 - What's So Scary?

Discuss scary situations and discuss girls' fears about sharing Jesus with others.

Sometimes girls are more willing to start off with discussion instead of an activity. This step will help them build relationships by sharing some of their fears. Ahead of time, make multiple sets of index cards that include questions about fear like: *What's the scariest amusement park ride you've ever been on? What's the scariest movie you've ever seen? What are you most afraid of?* Add more question cards as needed. Divide students into groups of three or four and give each group one of the cards. Each student should answer the question. Rotate the cards around the groups. Before moving on, ask for volunteers to answer this question: **What scares you about sharing Jesus with your friends?** *(Needed: index cards, pens.)*

Step 4 - Bandages

Apply Scripture "Bandages" to case study situations.

Teen girls love solving problems. With that in mind, help students get even more in depth with the Step 4 activity. You may want to have a few concordances handy. Make sure students know how to use them. After students listen to the three monologues (as directed in Step 4), have them look up Scripture that would encourage and support one or more of the three characters. Pass out three bandage strips to each girl. Have them write the Scripture references they've found on the bandages and give them to the appropriate character. Point out that what most unbelieving people need to know most is that Jesus can help them heal where they hurt—somewhat like bandages. *(Needed: Bibles, concordances, bandages.)*

MOSTLY GUYS

Step 1 - Walk the Walk

Navigate an obstacle course while carrying one teammate.

Guys and roleplays are not always a great mix. Instead, give your guys a physical challenge. Divide into groups of five and in each group, designate one guy to be the "paralytic" and the other four to be his "Stretcher Friends." The friends must carry the paralytic through a course that you lay out ahead of time. Make sure the course is difficult enough to be challenging. Discuss: **How did you like that activity? Was it difficult? Did you get tired? Did you ever resent your friend or the fact that you had to carry him? How can we "carry" our friends who don't know Jesus? How might they feel similar to how the "paralytic" felt in this exercise? What feelings do you have about sharing your faith with your friends that compare to what you felt during this exercise?**

Step 4 - Video Testimonies

Videotape students' testimonies.

Have students make videotapes of their testimonies—one or two minute personal stories about what Christ has done in their lives. *(Needed: TV, VCR, tape.)*

Step 5 - Wallet Reminders

Make prayer cards that fit in guys' wallets.

Follow the directions for Step 5 up to the point where students write their friends' names on index cards. Instead, bring in blank business cards (or paper cut to that size). Have students write the names down on these cards to keep in their wallets. This might be a less intimidating idea for guys than taping cards to a cross. *(Needed: blank business cards or business card-sized paper, paper, pens.)*

EXTRA FUN

Step 1 - Gurney Races

Teams race on hospital gurneys.

Have teams race around a course carrying one team member on a hospital gurney. These are a little hard to come by. But if you ask a local hospital community relations department, you might be able to borrow two gurneys. Make a course in a gym or outside using cones or chairs as turn-around points. Have teams race head-to-head, or have them go one at a time. (This latter option makes the fun possible even if you can only get one gurney). If you are unable to get a gurney from a hospital, consider renting one for a day from a hospital equipment rental store. *(Needed: hospital gurneys.)*

Step 5 - Party Planning

Plan an Extra Fun party for the friends your students listed in Step 5.

After you finish the cross exercise in Step 5, have your kids plan a party. The party's goal might be: 1) To review the things learned during this friendship series, or 2) To invite the visitors your students wrote down in Step 5. If your group is small, involve everyone in the planning of every aspect. If your group is more than a dozen kids, divide them into smaller groups to plan different aspects of the party: games, decorations, food, entertainment.

OPTIONS

SESSION FIVE

Step 1 - TV Clips

Show clips from a hospital TV show.

Record on your VCR clips from movies or TV shows that feature emergency room scenes of doctors saving lives. Show the video, then discuss: **Why do you think the characters were motivated to save lives? Do you think they cared about the people they were saving?** Help students see that people who don't know Jesus are in an "emergency" situation—their eternities hang in the balance. Discuss how students can be used by God to help "save" their friends who don't know Jesus. *(Needed: TV, VCR, home video of TV clips.)*

Step 2 - Faces in the Crowd

Show a video to provoke students to think about sharing their faith.

Gather up recent yearbooks from the schools your students attend. Film 2-5 second clips of a number of faces. If possible, intersperse these clips with one or two teens stating common objections to sharing their faith: *I don't want to judge them; they have their own beliefs; who am I to tell them what to do?* When you show the clips, play a song in the background that motivates students to introduce others to Jesus. Discuss: **Do you really think *everyone* needs Jesus? Do you think Jesus could make your friends' lives better? Why or why not? Why is sharing our faith so hard?** *(Needed: TV, VCR, video segment, CD player, CD.)*

Step 1 - Free Candy!

Give away free candy in the beginning instead of in the middle of the lesson.

Step 3 in the main lesson calls for one student to interrupt the class by shouting, "There's free candy!" If you do this to start your lesson, you'll not only have a succinct introduction to today's theme, you'll also shave some time off of Step 3. Discuss: **Do you appreciate the fact that (name of person who announced the free candy) decided to share with others instead of keeping it all to herself? We have Great News about Jesus. Are you going to keep that to yourself or share it with others?** *(Needed: candy bars.)*

Step 2 - Introduction Stories

Students talk about how they were introduced to Christ.

Ahead of time, ask two students to share about how they came to know Jesus and about the stretcher friends who were involved. Try to find two students who have different stories about how they were introduced to Jesus. When they finish, ask if anyone else would like to share how they were introduced to Jesus. Discuss: **What's the best way to introduce someone to Jesus? What ways are effective? What ways aren't? Why?**

Steps 4/5 - Simulation Stories

Instead of using Resource 11, write hypothetical stories of teens who come to Christ.

Instead of choosing volunteers to read the monologues off Resource 11, make up your own story simulations to read. Find out ahead of time what the names and needs are of some of the unchurched peers in your students' circle of influence. Write and then read hypothetical stories about how they came to know Christ and the difference it made to them. Follow the directions for Step 5 here as written in the lesson.

Step 2 - Geeks for God

Discuss some uniquely urban issues concerning evangelism.

Sometimes the pressure involved in taking a stand for Jesus can be more intense in urban areas. Peers may call your students "God Nerd" or "Whacked Hallelujah Freak." Discuss: **Are you willing to look like a geek in the eyes of some in order to serve Jesus? What will the consequences be of sharing your faith?** Be aware that in some cases it may be physically dangerous to share one's faith. Help students work through this critical issue, then use Step 2 as written in the lesson. *(Needed: see Step 2.)*

Step 3 - An Inexpensive Option

Substitute candy for candy bars in Step 3.

If you are working with a super-low budget try using a bag of marshmallows, candy corn, or Hershey's Kisses in Step 3.

Step 5 - Hip Hop Party

Use urban music to celebrate friendship.

Have teens bring in their favorite Christian hip-hop, rap, and gospel music (like Kirk Franklin, Out of Eden, Hezekiah Walker, etc.) Celebrate all five of the friendship lessons they've learned in this series. Make a party of it—don't forget refreshments and decorations. Have a "rap off" and see which teen can put together the best lyrics on the five types of friendship. Give a prize to the winner. Further, give a prize to those who can "break off somethin' proper" [translation: put the best music together] using the following styles for the following types of friendship:

- Extreme Friend Rap
- Bleacher Friend Rasta
- Second-Chance Friend Hip-Hop
- Fox-Hole Friend Blues
- Stretcher Friend Gospel Music

(Needed: CD and/or cassette player, music students bring in.)

JR. HIGH / HIGH SCHOOL COMBINED

STEP 3 - $10 GIVEAWAY

Give away $10 instead of candy bars.

Instead of offering free candy bars, have a student interrupt your meeting and yell, "I'll give $10 to the first person who shakes my hand!" The $10 prize is certain to get the interest of your older students. *(Needed: $10 bill.)*

STEP 4 - BRING HIM UP

Practice brining up the subject of Jesus while roleplaying various conversations.

Here's a practical way to get both middle school and high school students to practice sharing their faith: Read the following quotes then have volunteers suggest ways to follow-up with a comment that would bring up Jesus. Statements:

• "I don't know what to do! My mom's having surgery tomorrow. I'm really scared." (Possible response: "Can I pray for you?")

• "Allison's so mean. I think I hate her. How can you still be polite to her after all she's said about you?" (Possible response: "I've said things that are stupid, too. But God keeps loving me and wants me to keep loving others.")

SIXTH GRADE

STEP 2 - OBVIOUS EVIDENCE

Design and produce a commercial for Jesus.

The learning ability of most sixth graders is enhanced when they use a variety of senses in the learning process. Plan ahead of time for the students to create and film a TV commercial no longer than 2-3 minutes. The commercial should explain why Jesus is the best friend for anyone who doesn't know Him. Have the students first prepare a script that includes information, such as: **What is it like to be Jesus' friend? What are the benefits of having Jesus for a friend? What are the disadvantages when you don't know Jesus?** Show the commercial to the entire class. *(Needed: TV, VCR, video camera and tape.)*

STEP 4 - ROLEPLAY IT

Use roleplays about sharing faith.

Instead of writing responses to Resource 12, have students roleplay possible conversations with the characters on that sheet. How might they start a conversation? How could they find a way to introduce what Jesus had to offer? Let as many volunteers roleplay these situations as you have time for. You may want to play the part of the characters from Resource 11 during the roleplays. Give students feedback. *(Needed: copies of Resource 11.)*

PLANNING CHECKLIST

STEP 1 (5-10 MIN. UNLESS NOTED)

- ❑ **Extra Action:** Hoop It Up (10-15 min.)
- ❑ **Small Group:** Picture This!
- ❑ **Large Group:** Stretcher Races
- ❑ **Mostly Girls:** What's So Scary?
- ❑ **Mostly Guys:** Walk the Walk
- ❑ **Extra Fun:** Gurney Races
- ❑ **Media:** TV Clips
- ❑ **Short Time:** Free Candy!

STEP 2 (10-15 MIN. UNLESS NOTED)

- ❑ **Large Group:** Life without Jesus?
- ❑ **Heard It All:** EMT Visit
- ❑ **Little Bible:** The Greatest Love
- ❑ **Fellowship & Worship:** Show and Tell
- ❑ **Media:** Faces in the Crowd
- ❑ **Short Time:** Introduction Stories (5 min.)
- ❑ **Urban:** Geeks for God
- ❑ **Sixth Grade:** Obvious Evidence

STEP 3 (15-20 MIN. UNLESS NOTED)

- ❑ **Little Bible:** Living Water Anyone?
- ❑ **Urban:** An Inexpensive Option
- ❑ **Combined:** $10 Giveaway

STEP 4 (10-15 MIN. UNLESS NOTED)

- ❑ **Small Group:** Testimonies
- ❑ **Large Group:** Group Variation
- ❑ **Mostly Girls:** Bandages
- ❑ **Mostly Guys:** Video Testimonies
- ❑ **Short Time:** Simulation Stories*
- ❑ **Combined:** Bring Him Up
- ❑ **Sixth Grade:** Roleplay It

STEP 5 (5-10 MIN. UNLESS NOTED)

- ❑ **Extra Action:** Shout Tag
- ❑ **Heard It All:** Introduction Night
- ❑ **Fellowship & Worship:** Prayer, Nail, Song (10-15 min.)
- ❑ **Mostly Guys:** Wallet Reminders
- ❑ **Extra Fun:** Party Planning
- ❑ **Urban:** Hip Hop Party

* two combined steps

Other Custom Curriculum Titles

High School

Beliefs to Beware of — Straight Answers about Cults
Can't Help It? — How to Quit Bad Habits and Start Good Ones
Free Gifts for Everybody! — Discovering Your Spiritual Gifts
Going Against the Flow — When Being a Christian Feels Weird
Hormone Helper — Getting Along as a Guy or Girl
Is Anybody There? — Reaching for a Real Relationship with God
Streetwise — Great Advice from Proverbs and Ecclesiastes
NEW! ***The Drug Free Challenge*** — Surviving as a Christian in a World Fried by Drugs and Alcohol
The Whole Story — Things They Don't Tell You in School about Sex, and More!
They're Not Like Us! — What Different Churches Believe
Too Tough? — The Hardest Teachings of Jesus
Unseen Mysteries — A Behind-the-Scenes Look at Angels, Demons, and More
What Do You Think? — Measuring Your Opinions against the Bible
What, Me Holy? — Staying Clean in a Grungy World
Your Bible's Alive — How to Get Friendly with God's Book
You've Got Style — Choosing Your Music, Clothes, and Attitude

Junior High/Middle School

Basic Training — Things Every Christian Kid Should Know
Bouncing Back — What to Do after Mistakes, Embarrassment, and Other Daily Disasters
Extreme Closeup — How You and God Can Stay Connected
Face to Face with Jesus — What He's Really Like
Gotta Have It? — How to Get What You Need and Forget What You Don't
In the Beginning . . . What? — The Bible Talks about Creation
Just Look at You — Feeling Good about the Way You're Made
New Testament Speedway — A Zip through the New Testament
Old Testament Speedway — A Zip through the Old Testament
Parent Pains — Bringing Some Peace to Your Place
Riding Those Mood Swings — What to Do with Up-and-Down Feelings
Tongue Untwisters — Keeping Your Mouth from Getting You in Trouble
What Would Jesus Do? — Making the Best Choices
Which Way to God? — What Other Religions Believe
Why Be a Christian? — Deciding Whether It's Worth Following Jesus

To order, call David C. Cook Ministry Resources at 1-800-323-7543 (U.S.)
In Canada call 1-800-263-2664

NAME____________________________

STREET__________________________

CITY____________________________

STATE__________ ZIP____________

NO POSTAGE NECESSARY IF MAILED IN THE UNITED STATES

BUSINESS REPLY MAIL

FIRST CLASS MAIL PERMIT NO.720 COLORADO SPRINGS, CO

POSTAGE WILL BE PAID BY ADDRESSEE

David C. Cook Church Ministries
ATTN: YOUTH DEPT.
4050 LEE VANCE VIEW
COLORADO SPRINGS, CO 80918-9951

(tape here)

6. What did you like best about this course?

7. What suggestions do you have for improving Custom Curriculum?

8. Other topics you'd like to see covered in this series:

9. Are you?
   - ❑ Full-time, paid youthworker
   - ❑ Part-time, paid youthworker
   - ❑ Volunteer youthworker

10. When did you use Custom Curriculum?
   - ❑ Sunday School ❑ Small Group
   - ❑ Youth Group ❑ Retreat
   - ❑ Other

11. What grades did you use it with? ____________

12. How many kids used the curriculum in an average week? ____________

13. What's the approximate attendance of your entire Sunday school program (Nursery through Adult)? ____________

14. If you would like information on other Custom Curriculum courses, or other youth products from Cook Ministry Resources, please fill out the following:

Name: ____________________

Church Name: ____________________

Address: ____________________

____

Phone: (______) ____________________

Thank you!

Custom Curriculum Critique

Please take a moment to fill out this evaluation form, rip it out, fold it, tape it, and send it back to us. This will help us continue to customize products for you. Thanks!

1. Overall, please give this *Custom Curriculum* course (*Extreme Friendship)* a grade in terms of how well it worked for you. (A=excellent; B=above average; C=average; D=below average; F=failure) Circle one.

A B C D F

2. Now assign a grade to each part of this curriculum that you used.

a. Upfront article	A	B	C	D	F	Didn't use
b. Publicity Clip art	A	B	C	D	F	Didn't use
c. Resource Sheets	A	B	C	D	F	Didn't use
d. Session 1	A	B	C	D	F	Didn't use
e. Session 2	A	B	C	D	F	Didn't use
f. Session 3	A	B	C	D	F	Didn't use
g. Session 4	A	B	C	D	F	Didn't use
h. Session 5	A	B	C	D	F	Didn't use

3. How helpful were the options?

❑ Very helpful
❑ Somewhat helpful
❑ Not too helpful
❑ Not at all helpful

4. Rate the amount of options:

❑ Too many
❑ About the right amount
❑ Too few

5. Tell us how often you used each type of option (4=Always; 3=Sometimes; 2=Seldom; 1=Never)

	4	3	2	1
Extra Action	❑	❑	❑	❑
Combined Jr. High/High School	❑	❑	❑	❑
Urban	❑	❑	❑	❑
Small Group	❑	❑	❑	❑
Large Group	❑	❑	❑	❑
Extra Fun	❑	❑	❑	❑
Heard It All Before	❑	❑	❑	❑
Little Bible Background	❑	❑	❑	❑
Short Meeting Time	❑	❑	❑	❑
Fellowship and Worship	❑	❑	❑	❑
Mostly Guys	❑	❑	❑	❑
Mostly Girls	❑	❑	❑	❑
Media	❑	❑	❑	❑
Extra Challenge (High School only)	❑	❑	❑	❑
Sixth Grade (Jr. High/M.S. only)	❑	❑	❑	❑